四十七世天童宏智禪師

Traditional Chinese Woodcut
of Zen Master Hongzhi

CULTIVATING THE EMPTY FIELD

The Silent Illumination of
Zen Master Hongzhi

—

Translated by Taigen Daniel Leighton
with Yi Wu
Foreword by Tenshin Anderson

San Francisco 1991
NORTH POINT PRESS

LIBRARY OF CONGRESS
CATALOGING-IN-PUBLICATION DATA

Cheng-chüeh, 1091–1157.
    Cultivating the empty field : the silent illumination
of Zen Master Hongzhi / translated by Taigen
Daniel Leighton with Yi Wu ; foreword by Tenshin
Anderson.
        p.   cm.
    Translated from Chinese.
    Includes bibliographical references.
    ISBN 0-86547-474-5. — ISBN 0-86547-475-3 (pbk.)
    1. Enlightenment (Zen Buddhism)—Early works
to 1800.   2. Meditation—Zen Buddhism—Early
works to 1800.   I. Leighton, Taigen Daniel.
II. Wu, I., 1939–   .   III. Title.
BQ9288.C44   1991
181'.043927—dc20   90-20842

The true form is magnificently illuminated with gleaming fire.
The teaching's voice is total silence amid the ringing wind chimes.
The moon hangs in the old pine tree, cold in the falling night.
The chilled crane in its nest in the clouds has not yet been aroused
   from its dreams.

HONGZHI, Homage to the Fourth Ancestor

A person of the Way fundamentally does not dwell anywhere.
The white clouds are fascinated with the green mountain's
foundation. The bright moon cherishes being carried along with
the flowing water. The clouds part and the mountain appears.
The moon sets and the water is cool. Each bit of autumn contains
vast interpenetration without bounds.

HONGZHI, Practice Instructions

CONTENTS

CONTENTS

FOREWORD

Homage to Shakyamuni Buddha.
Homage to the succession of Indian founders and Zen pioneers in
the Way up to the present.
Homage to Tiantong Hongzhi, the author of this book.

Hongzhi said, "Empty and desireless, cold and thin, simple and genuine, this is how to strike down and fold up the remaining habits of many lives. When the stains from old habits are exhausted, the original light appears, blazing through your skull, not admitting any other matters. Vast and spacious, like sky and water merging during autumn, like snow and moon having the same color, this field is without boundary, beyond direction, magnificently one entity without edge or seam. Further, when you turn within and drop off everything completely, realization occurs. Right at the time of entirely dropping off, deliberation and discussion are one thousand or ten thousand miles away. Still no principle is discernible, so what could there be to point to or explain? People with the bottom of the bucket fallen out immediately find total trust. So we are told simply to realize mutual response and explore mutual response, then turn around and enter the world. Roam and play in *samādhi*. Every detail clearly appears before you. Sound and form, echo and shadow, happen instantly without leaving traces."

This teaching speaks for itself. I need not add to it. I will only say that I am most moved and grateful for these sublime encouragements.

With this book, much of the great teacher Hongzhi's *Extensive Record* is now available in our language. Now we English speakers can hear the blessing of this genuine practice lineage of Buddhas and Zen founders. Step by step our language is becoming a medium to express the Buddha's teaching. This translation has significantly expanded our literary sources for an important field of study and practice—silent illumination. Perhaps it will clarify some common confusions about silent illumination in Zen. Please enjoy reading Hongzhi's words.

Rev. Taigen Dan Leighton and Prof. Yi Wu have worked long and hard, with great energy and devotion, to create this translation. I feel proud and deeply grateful for what they have produced. I also wish to acknowledge and thank North Point Press for its ongoing commitment to publishing the root texts of Zen.

I joyfully look forward to generations of Western Zen students having the opportunity to thoroughly study this wonderful book. I am inspired and happy that this text is available to those who are dedicated to living the way of Zen. Without exception, anyone who has real communion with an authentic lineage of Buddhas and Zen adepts is bound to become liberated. May these teachings bring welfare to all living beings everywhere.

Tenshin Anderson, Abbot
Green Dragon Temple
Green Gulch Farm, December 1990

PREFACE

The writings of the twelfth-century Chan Master Hongzhi Zhengjue are poetic expressions of meditative concentration and insight, and of the working of awakened mind. These rich and dense teachings might be read most usefully as one reads poetry. Hongzhi employed a style more holographic than the rational, expository style of Western thought; each of his paragraphs encapsulates the whole teaching. This material is both spiritual literature and meditation instruction, to be deliberately savored, digested, and nourished by.

As well as being evocative literature, Hongzhi's writings are also instructions in meditative practice for students seeking to realize Zen (Chan) truth. They can assist us in the techniques and actualization of spiritual life. His method of presentation allows beneficial attitudes and insights to filter through our habitual conditioned viewpoints and so help the process of realignment with our inherent luminous true nature. These practice instructions are guides to consciousness at the unified, illuminating source of creation, and also to appropriate responsive interaction amid the human world of desire and confusion.

Hongzhi was the first master fully to articulate silent illumination, a form of nondual objectless meditation in which the essence of Buddhist truth is experienced. Called "just sitting" in Japan, this practice has striking similarities to the Tibetan *Mahāmudrā* and *Dzogchen,* other examples of nondualistic meditation teachings in the Buddhist tradition. Hongzhi is of paramount importance in the history of the development of Chan/Zen meditation practice, particularly as a primary precursor of the famed Japanese Zen pioneer Dōgen.

Hongzhi left a vast body of writings celebrated for their eloquence, which were preserved by his disciples in the *Extensive Record of Chan Master Hongzhi.* Composed of nine volumes, these writings include poetry, sermons, informal talks and sayings, instructions to individual students, and collections of old teaching stories. Herein is a translation of volume six, the Practice Instructions, along with a selection of Religious Verses from volume eight. An introduction presents approaches to Hongzhi's teaching and provides background for his life and work.

Hongzhi's writings, with their inspiring vision of the essence and potential of the universal spirit, have previously been available in English only in scattered fragments. I hope that this volume will serve as a comprehensive introduction to Hongzhi for interested Westerners.

The Practice Instructions are presented in the fifty-six paragraphs of the Chinese original. I have drawn headings for each paragraph from the text. The titles and subheadings of the Religious Verses, however, are all by Hongzhi himself. Bracketed material in the text indicates interpolations deemed necessary for clarity, for example, unstated subjects.

All Chinese terms and names in the text are spelled with the contemporary Pinyin transliteration system, except for titles of

English works that use the older Wade-Giles system. With a few exceptions Pinyin transliteration is pronounced approximately as it appears. All grouped vowels are diphthongs. "C" is pronounced like the "ts" in tsetse fly. "Q" is pronounced like the "ch" in chuckle. "X" is pronounced like the "s" in sugar. "Zh" is pronounced like the "dg" in fudging. The equivalent Wade Giles transliteration for Chinese names is provided in Appendix C.

I would like to express my deep appreciation to Yi Wu, Professor of Chinese Language at the California Institute of Integral Studies in San Francisco. He reviewed the first stage of translation with me to clarify questions of vocabulary and grammar and to verify accuracy. Yi Wu informed the translation not only with his linguistic understanding, but also with his expert knowledge of classical Chinese wisdom and literature.

I am grateful to Mark Tatz, Rina Sircar, and Jim Mitchell for careful reading and suggestions, and to Rosalind Leighton for adept editorial aid. Indispensable assistance and encouragement was rendered in various ways by Paul Schwartz, Marty Wolfe, Lou and Blanche Hartman, Kazuaki Tanahashi, Linda Hess, Stephen Colgan, and Jack Earley. Thanks to Bhikksu Heng Shen of Gold Mountain Monastery in San Francisco, who provided the drawing of Hongzhi. Thanks also to Gary Snyder for encouraging publication of this book, and to Jack Shoemaker, Barbara Ras, and the people at North Point Press for their strong support.

I especially dedicate this work to Rev. Kando Nakajima, who firmly set me on the path of just sitting, to Tenshin Reb Anderson for his whole-hearted patience and guidance, and to Thomas Cleary, to whom all English-speaking students of East Asian wisdom are immeasurably indebted.

Hongzhi's disciple Puqung, the compiler of volume six of the

Extensive Record, asks in his preface for the reader to excuse his attempt to record Hongzhi's talks, given the shallowness of his own realization compared to that of his master. How much more must a modern translator apologize, separated from Hongzhi not only by depths of realization and eight and a half centuries, but also by the difference between Chinese and English! Despite the inevitable inadequacies of such translation, even at its best, this attempt is offered with the faith that Hongzhi's expression of clear radiant mind will shine through and will still have the capacity to guide and inspire spiritual practitioners in realizing their own omnipresent illuminating mind.

Taigen Dan Leighton

INTRODUCTION

The silent illumination that Zen Master Hongzhi expounds is both a form of sitting meditation practice and an orientation to spiritual way of life. His meditation instructions do not specify yogic postures or rituals such as would have been familiar to his students at the temple where he taught. Instead his writings display the many facets of the universally available experience of nondual objectless meditation and the endless refinements and attunements involved in living out this awareness.

Most traditional meditation, both Buddhist and non-Buddhist, consists of concentration on specific objects such as visual images, sounds, breathing, concepts, stories, or deities in order to develop heightened states of concentrated awareness called *samādhi*. Silent illumination, however, involves withdrawal from exclusive focus on a particular sensory or mental object to allow intent apprehension of all phenomena as a unified totality. This objectless meditation aims at a radical, refined nondualism that does not grasp at any of the highly subtle distinctions to which our familiar mental workings are prone and which estrange us from our experience. Such subject-object dichotomization is understood as artificial, a fabrication.

Silent illumination is also objectless in the sense of not seeking after specific limited goals. The ultimate purpose of spiritual practice, universally awakened heart/mind, cannot be set apart from our own inherent being and our immediate, moment-to-moment awareness. As Hongzhi emphasizes, the entire practice rests on the faith, verified in experience, that the field of vast brightness is ours from the outset. The practitioner's exertion and dedication are devoted to manifesting this ultimate truth with constancy right in ordinary existence. Silent illumination is thus fully experienced in meditative contemplation, and then naturally expressed in sincere compassionate behavior in the world.

Hongzhi's expression of silent illumination is the culmination of a sophisticated Zen Buddhist teaching tradition inspired by the founders of the Chinese Caodong lineage (pronounced "tsow-dong"), later called Sōtō in Japan. (Although Hongzhi was Chinese, Japanese terms such as "Zen" and "Sōtō," which are more commonly known in the West, will be generally used in this work for the sake of clarity.) This Chinese Sōtō tradition developed a theoretical understanding through the dialectic of insight into universal truth and its interplay with the particulars of the phenomenal world. A corresponding practice model was enacted with the dialectic between meditative introspection and naturally appropriate activity in everyday life. Hongzhi's Practice Instructions are the graceful and subtle expression of the fruition of this tradition. His work was later elaborated and developed in Japan by Zen Master Dōgen and the Sōtō tradition that derived from him.

Hongzhi's silent illumination is of great relevance to contemporary spiritual seekers. His teachings are important as a primary source for Dōgen, whose work remains highly influential to Zen practice. Even more, Hongzhi is valuable to us as a lucid guide, beyond any particular tradition, to the subtleties of spiritual awareness and its life in the world.

Hongzhi's vast luminous buddha field is the field of buddha nature, our inalienable endowment of wisdom. Hongzhi tells us that this bright empty field, which lies immanent in us all, can in no way be cultivated or artificially enhanced. We must only recognize it and not allow our busy, mischievous thinking and conditioning to interfere with our own radiant clarity.

Hongzhi's Life

Hongzhi Zhengjue (1091–1157) was born in Xijou in present-day Shansi Province, to a family named Li.[1] Although Hongzhi, or "Vast Wisdom," was a posthumous name bestowed by the emperor, in the interest of clarity and consistency it is used throughout this work. During his life he would have been called Zhengjue and later Tiantong Zhengjue: Zhengjue, "Correct (or True) Awakening," was his monk ordination name, and Tiantong was the mountain where his temple stood. In Japanese Hongzhi is known as Wanshi Shōgaku, the Japanese pronunciation of the Chinese characters for Hongzhi Zhengjue.

Hongzhi was a very intelligent child, memorizing several thousand characters before he was seven years old. His father, Congdao, was a lay disciple of Desun, who was in turn a disciple of Huanglong Huinan (d. 1069), a founder of one of the two main branches of Linji Chan.[2] Desun was impressed with Congdao's son and predicted that he would become a vessel of dharma, one who realizes and transmits the teaching of truth.

When he was eleven, Hongzhi left home to become a monk. At

eighteen he went to Rujou in modern Honan Province to study with the Sōtō Zen master Kumu Faqeng (1071–1128). Kumu's style of practice involved sitting meditation so still that his body was said to resemble a block of dry wood, hence his name, which means "Dry Wood Complete Dharma." Hongzhi emulated this practice of upright, immobile meditation throughout his career. Such cross-legged sitting in lotus posture is the fundamental practice for the Sōtō tradition, the unstated physical context for Hongzhi's meditation instructions.

After a few years Hongzhi traveled to other temples. At Shangshan (Incense Mountain) Temple, Hongzhi overheard a monk reciting the line from the Flower Ornament Sutra, "The eyes which our parents give us can behold three thousand worlds." Upon hearing this, Hongzhi experienced an awakening.[3]

When Hongzhi told Master Shangshan (as often happened, the abbot was known by the name of the temple) of his experience, Shangshan pointed to a box of incense and asked, "What is inside?" Hongzhi said, "What does Mind do?" Shangshan asked, "Where does your enlightenment come from?" Hongzhi drew a circle in the air with his hand and threw it behind him. Shangshan said, "You are a man who produces muddiness. What is your capacity?" Hongzhi said, "Mistake." Shangshan said, "Don't show other people," and Hongzhi answered, "Yes, yes."

Such dialogues have their own logic, and function most effectively with minimal explanation. Hongzhi's response to Shangshan about the incense box reflects his understanding of the total interpenetration of mind and phenomena. Later Dōgen would echo Hongzhi when he called his own life "one continuous mistake."

Hongzhi left Shangshan and, at age twenty-three, arrived at the temple of Danxia Zichun (1054–1119). Danxia asked him, "What is your self before the empty *kalpa?*"[4] Hongzhi said, "A frog in a well swallows the moon; at midnight I do not borrow a lantern." Danxia said, "Not yet." As Hongzhi was about to respond, Danxia beat him with his whisk, then asked, "You still say you do not borrow?" Hongzhi experienced some understanding and bowed. Danxia said, "Why don't you make a statement?" Hongzhi said, "Today I lost money and was punished." Danxia said, "I have no time to beat you up."

Hongzhi's response about not borrowing a lantern at midnight expresses the Sōtō sense of the interfusion of light and darkness. Right in the blackness of merging with emptiness, the light of differentiation naturally emerges. Furthermore, in the introspective withdrawal from attachment to sense phenomena, one's own inner illumination appears. Hongzhi's response also refers to the story of a monk departing from his teacher in the middle of the night. The teacher handed the student a lantern but then, as the student started into the dark, blew out the flame, whereupon the student was awakened. Danxia, however, did not accept Hongzhi's first answer and picked up on his word "borrow" to emphasize the student's relationship to the teacher and the necessity of intimately experiencing the truth.

Danxia Zichun was a dharma-brother of Hongzhi's former teacher Kumu, both disciples of the famed master Furong Daokai (1043–1118). A couple of generations after the Sōtō Zen transmission almost died out, Furong revitalized the school, establishing strong standards for the monastic community. Furong refused the offer of elaborate honors from the emperor as being inappropriate for a monk, which led to his being exiled for a number of years. This model of integrity greatly impressed Hongzhi, whose poem praising Furong may be found in the Religious Verses below.

Hongzhi spent several years studying with Danxia Zichun, following him when Danxia moved from his temple on Danxia Mountain in Honan to Mount Daqeng and later to Mount Dehong in Hupei. In both places he took the position of "first seat" as Danxia's teaching assistant. Before Danxia's death in 1119 Hongzhi received his seal of transmission, which certified Hongzhi's understanding and qualification to teach the dharma.

Hongzhi then lived in various temples, including visits to Chenju Juyuan Monastery on Yunju Mountain in Kiangsi, where Yuanwu Keqin (1063–1135) was teaching. Yuanwu's famed collection of one hundred stories with commentary, the *Blue Cliff Record*, is one of the most frequently used sources for Zen meditative study of the dialogues and stories of the old masters, called *kung-an* in Chinese and *kōan* in Japanese (literally, "public cases").[5] Hongzhi's study with Yuanwu probably gave him some familiarity with formal koan practice as done in the Rinzai school of that time. Hongzhi later compiled his own collections of old koans, one of which became the basis for the popular *Book of Serenity*.

In 1129, Hongzhi accepted an invitation to teach at the Jingde (Bright Virtue) Monastery on Mount Tiantong in Ming Province in modern Zhejiang. When Hongzhi arrived, the Jingde Monastery was small and in disrepair. Under Hongzhi's supervision, the temple was reconstructed and eventually accommodated twelve hundred monks. Its huge meditation hall could hold all the monks drawn to his rich teaching. Hongzhi seems to have been unflappable amid the difficulties of this expansion. The Japanese Sōtō successor Eihei Dōgen (1200–1253) tells the story about a time when Hongzhi's monastery had provisions for a thousand monks, and fifteen or sixteen hundred had gathered. An officer of the temple implored Hongzhi to send away the extra monks. Hongzhi resolutely replied that "each of them has his own mouth. It is not your concern. Do not worry about it."[6] Dōgen commends Hongzhi's faith in sincere practice as the essential affair.

This was a period of political and social turmoil in China, often accompanied by sporadic disruptions of agriculture and widespread hunger. Although it was no longer the custom in Zen temples, Hongzhi himself took no food after noon. On various occasions he donated food from the temple supply to nearby villagers, thereby saving many lives.

From his arrival in 1129 Hongzhi remained on Mount Tiantong, refusing all invitations to leave. He was widely learned, accomplished in Confucian and other Chinese cultural lore, and was able to apply his erudition and eloquence to the teaching of Zen practice. He articulated the meditation praxis of the Sōtō tradition in his teaching of silent illumination, formulating the guideposts for meditation in this tradition as Furong had for monastic community life.

In autumn 1157 Hongzhi journeyed down the mountain for the first time in nearly thirty years. He visited local military and government officials and lay patrons of his temple to say goodbye and thank them for their support. He returned to Jingde Temple on November tenth and the next morning bathed, put on fresh robes, and went to the dharma (lecture) hall, where he gave a farewell talk to his monks. He asked his attendant for a brush and wrote a letter to his colleague and sometime critic, the Zen teacher Dahui Zonggao (1089–1163),[7] asking him to take charge of the temple. Then Hongzhi wrote:

Illusory dreams, phantom flowers—
Sixty-seven years.
A white bird vanishes in the mist,
Autumn waters merge with the sky.[8]

He then passed away in formal meditation position. It is said that his body remained fresh in its coffin for seven days.

Six months later the Southern Song Emperor Gaocong gave him the posthumous title Hongzhi Chanshi, "Chan Master Vast Wisdom." Hongzhi's immediate influence was maintained through his numerous direct successors, eight of whom merited their own biographies in the *Five Lamps Merged in the Source*, a thirteenth-century abridged compilation of five major Zen history texts.[9]

The Sōtō Context

Hongzhi's practice of silent illumination includes a strong, though implicit, devotional element: reverence, expressed in his writings through his great appreciation of nature, and gratitude, apparent in his respect for the lineage of teachers who have transmitted the practice. Especially he venerates the great Ancestors, the founding figures in the lineage who established or enriched the tradition, and to whom Hongzhi addressed some of his verses. Hongzhi's personal attitude of "serving the ancestors" is concretized generally in Zen temples with the daily ritual recitation of the names in the lineage reaching back to Shākyamuni Buddha.

Hongzhi's Practice Instructions can be more fully appreciated if it is understood how they echo and synthesize the root teachings of the Caodong/Sōtō lineage. Particularly important to a comprehension of Hongzhi's philosophy and vocabulary are the works of Shitou and Dongshan and their teachings regarding the interplay of absolute and relative, which Dongshan formulated in the five ranks.

The Sōtō lineage descended from the famed Sixth Ancestor of Zen, Dajian Huineng (638–713), through his second-generation successor Shitou Xiqian (700–790). Shitou and Mazu Dao-i (709–788), another second-generation descendant of Huineng, were the two great masters of their age in China from whom all later Zen descends.[10]

Hongzhi often refers to the teachings of Shitou, whose name means "Above the Rock," after a hut he built on a large boulder near his temple and in which he resided. Shitou was awakened when reading a passage by Sengzhao (374–414):[11] "The ultimate man is empty and hollow; he has no form, yet of the myriad things there is none that is not his own making. Who can understand myriad things as oneself? Only a sage." Thereupon Shitou said, "A sage has no self, yet there is nothing that is not himself."[12] From this insight into emptiness and interconnectedness Shitou formulated the basic theoretical principles of what came to be the Sōtō tradition in his classic long poem "Merging of Difference and Unity."[13]

"Merging" describes the dialectical interaction between the absolute, or universal, and the relative, or particulars. Although the poem is an expression of Shitou's personal insight, its categories of philosophical analysis derive from native Chinese Daoist yin-yang dialectics and, to a great extent, from the Chinese Huayen Buddhist dialectical system, extracted from the Huayen, or Flower Ornament Sutra. This sutra, the declaration of Shākyamuni Buddha upon his enlightenment, was incomprehensible to prospective students at Shākyamuni Buddha's time. Later, in East Asia, it was widely considered to be the loftiest expression of Buddhist philosophy. While the sutra itself is a highly visionary and exalted depiction of universal interdependence and of the vastness, power, and development of the activity of bodhisattvas (enlightening beings dedicated to universal awakening), the Chinese commentators derived from it many theoretical systems for classifying the stages and aspects of enlightened mind and teaching. Such systems as the Huayen fourfold *dharmadhatu*, or reality realm, were concerned with the relationship between principle and phenomena, and formed a basis for these Sōtō theories.

The interplay between absolute and relative more or less explicitly pervades all subsequent Sōtō teaching, including Hongzhi's, using various terminology as seems most helpful at the time. In "Merging of Difference and Unity," Shitou equates the absolute or universal with darkness (also sometimes called ultimate principle, unity, undifferentiated sameness, or what Shitou terms "the spiritual source"). The light, by contrast, signifies the relative or world of particulars; it is the light that differentiates phenomena, the "ten thousand" objectified things of the sense-desire realm. In addition to absolute and relative or universal and particular, these two aspects have also been called real and illusory, noumenal and phenomenal, true and partial, upright and inclined, straight and bent, equal and diverse, or empty and formed. They are analogous to the relationship between realization of truth and its functioning. The universal and particular have also been expressed in terms of the connection between host and guest, lord and vassal, black and white, subject and object, and yang and yin.

The full development of the relationship between absolute and relative is expounded in the five ranks (or degrees) teachings of Dongshan Liangjie (807–869), a third-generation successor to Shitou, in his poem "Song of the Jewel Mirror Samādhi" and in two sets of verse commentaries.[14] What came to be called the Caodong (Sōtō) school is named after Dongshan, combined with either the name Caoqi, the place where the Sixth Ancestor Huineng taught, or (according to some sources) the name of Caoshan Benji (840–901), one of Dongshan's most prominent disciples, who elaborated the theoretical side of the five ranks teaching.

Hongzhi speaks directly of the five ranks once in the Practice Instructions, referring to the "five levels of achievement" version of the teaching; his verse commentaries on the five ranks are included in the Religious Verses. The relationship between realization of the ultimate and functioning amid phenomena, a theme underlying all of the five ranks formulations, is clearly of central concern in Hongzhi's teaching. He plays with this theme through poetic nature metaphors and by encouraging and exhorting his listeners, and frequently describes the process and fulfillment of this integration of universality and particularity. For example:

> Where emptiness is empty it contains all of existence, where existence exists it joins the single emptiness. . . . The merging of sameness and difference becomes the entire creation's mother. This realm manifests the energy of the many thousands of beings.

The five ranks' embeddedness as a conceptual background for Sōtō praxis enactments and imagery requires their inclusion in any discussion of Hongzhi, and examples of each of the five ranks may be discerned throughout Hongzhi's Practice Instructions. The five ranks are, first, "the relative in the absolute," seeing phenomena against the backdrop of ultimate void; second, "the absolute in the relative," seeing the ultimate universal in each or any one phenomenal event; third, "coming from within the absolute," emerging silent and shining from the experiential state of union with the ultimate; fourth, "going within both absolute and relative," using both particulars and the sense of the universal with familiarity; and fifth, "arriving within both together," freely using either the phenomenal or the ineffable reality without attaching to either and without seeing them as separate. These five ranks represent ontological aspects of awakened mind more than stages of spiritual development.

Dongshan also presented a second, parallel system called the five degrees of meritorious achievement, which do reflect degrees of development of realization. These are conversion or intention (mindful commitment); service (obediently carrying out the practice); achievement (immersion in nondiscrimination); collective achievement (return to caring interaction with beings); and absolute achievement (individual beings and their universal interpenetrating connectedness seen as identical).

Although always philosophically relevant, the five ranks schemata have received varying emphasis in the tradition. The priority of actual practice has been asserted by figures such as Dōgen, who downplayed the five ranks, feeling that they encouraged fixation on an overly formulaic understanding. Indeed, the surviving Sōtō lineage descended from Dongshan's disciple Yunju Daoying (d. 902), who emphasized practice, rather than from Caoshan Benji, who promoted the five ranks teaching. Nevertheless, at different times Sōtō monks have continued to speculate about these teachings, following the various alternate formulations suggested by Caoshan. The five ranks also are considered one of the highest levels of koans, prior only to the precepts, in the Japanese Rinzai school's contemporary graded system of koans.[15]

Such systems of Buddhist phenomenology can seem abstract and esoteric, but Dongshan intended the five ranks for study in conjunction with practice. Hongzhi also echoes the practical teaching that Shitou developed, along with his insights into the absolute and relative. Traditional Buddhist practice involves transcending our attachment to desire objects, which results from the illusion of phenomena as inherently self-existent, separate, and alienated. This clinging is seen as the source of suffering. Yet Shitou's practice also seeks to transcend attachment to experiential realization of the ultimate. As he says, "Merging with principle is still not enlightenment."[16] The goal of Shitou's practice, as of Hongzhi's, is the full integration of deep experiential awareness of the ultimate source with our particular functioning amid worldly phenomena, referred to as being in the world but not of it.

Shitou articulated a practice model to lead to this integration in another long teaching poem, "Song of the Grass-Roof Hermitage" (see Appendix A). Here Shitou describes the establishment of a meditation practice/way of life that enables one to turn within to find the ultimate source and then return to the world to "relax completely; open your hands and walk, innocent." Shitou matches the ontological dialectic of integrating the absolute and relative with the practice dialectic summed up in the line "Turn around the light to shine within, then just return." This oscillation between realizing the ultimate, often actualized through meditation and in the monastic impulse, and functioning responsively in the world, often expressed with the bodhisattva model, becomes the paradigm for Sōtō practice. It is a pattern that Hongzhi demonstrates throughout his Practice Instructions.

The Sōtō tradition has evolved its own "family wind," or style, since Dongshan, having developed expedient teaching methodologies and surviving today in various manifestations in China,

Japan, and the West. One primary Sōtō teaching method is reflected in Hongzhi's frequent encouragement that practitioners embody the teaching with independence, illumining fully on their own. The awareness that nobody can experience the truth for another led to the characteristic Sōtō style of usually not giving explicit directions, leaving students to realize personally their own inmost nature. The central importance of this method is well illustrated in a story about Dongshan. When performing a memorial service for his teacher Yunyan Tansheng (781–841), Dongshan was asked by a monk why he so honored the relatively unknown Yunyan rather than other, more famous teachers Dongshan had studied with, such as Nanquan Puyuan (748–834) or Guishan Lingyou (771–853).[17] Dongshan answered that it was only because Yunyan had never directly explained anything to him.

Shining through the stories of Dongshan and his successors is the commitment to personal experience of the immanent presence of suchness, and the radical transcendence of all dualistic views, however subtle. When Dongshan was leaving Yunyan, he asked how to describe Yunyan's reality. Yunyan said, "Just this is it." After a pause, Yunyan added, "You are in charge of this great matter; you must be most thoroughgoing." Dongshan left and while crossing a stream saw his reflection. He was thoroughly enlightened and composed this verse:

> Just don't seek from others, or you'll be far estranged from Self.
> I now go on alone; everywhere I meet It:
> It now is me; I now am not It.
> One must understand in this way to merge with thusness.[18]

Hongzhi emphasizes the practical experiential enactment of this teaching of nondual awareness throughout his Practice Instructions.

Is Silent Illumination Quietistic?

Despite Hongzhi's extraordinary literary expression of dharma, he has been most noted in many historical surveys of Zen for an alleged dispute with the prominent Rinzai Zen teacher Dahui Zonggao. Dahui criticized silent illumination meditation as leading to excessive quietism and neglect of enlightenment. But Hongzhi and Dahui were actually friends who cooperated as teaching colleagues. Indeed, Dahui at times visited Hongzhi and sent students to him. Dahui's criticism was thus not directed personally at Hongzhi, but at some of his followers. Hongzhi in turn refrained from any comment on Dahui's criticism of his meditation teaching, and sent food to help Dahui's temple when it faced shortages. As previously mentioned, just before his death Hongzhi wrote a will requesting that Dahui take charge of his affairs.

Later adherents of the Rinzai (or Linji, named after the great, dynamic master Linji Yixuan [d. 867]) and Sōtō schools, as well as writers of Zen histories, sometimes made much of the supposed disagreement between Dahui and Hongzhi. But despite differing teaching styles and praxis emphases, Sōtō and Rinzai teachers have a tradition of cooperating in their work with students, as did their early progenitors Shitou and Mazu.[19] In fact, when the Sōtō lineage in China almost died out, it was preserved by a Rinzai master (see Appendix B, note 2). Eihei Dōgen, considered the founder of the Sōtō school in Japan, also succeeded to the Rinzai tradition in Japan before finding his Sōtō master in China, and later refused even to identify with such a thing as a "Zen school," much less Sōtō or Rinzai.

But even if the nature of his criticism has been distorted, the questions Dahui raised about silent illumination are very useful for examining the relevance and practicality of Hongzhi's teaching and seeing the possibilities for its misapplication. The issues and excesses that concerned Dahui are still alive in modern Zen practice, and can be seen reflected in potential imbalances in all spiritual traditions.

Instead of silent illumination, Dahui especially promoted the practice of meditation using koans as objects. Dahui's advocacy of intent contemplation of koans, aimed at dramatic opening and enlightenment experiences, was due largely to his own dedication to working not only with monks, but also with laypeople, including social and political leaders. Dahui encouraged laypeople to engage in personally transformative spiritual practice rather than merely subsidizing monastic institutions. Given the pressures of political and social upheaval facing his students, he believed that the dynamism of formal koan practice was more accessible to them than the less dramatic, traditional sitting meditation that was the format for silent illumination. He also believed koans more efficacious for awakening experiences, which he seems to have valued above the ongoing deepening and maturing of inherent awakening that silent illumination emphasizes.

Despite Dahui's new accentuation of them, the use of old teaching stories among Zen students goes back at least to the eighth century, used in various ways at different times in all branches of Zen. Although they have been more commonly associated with the Rinzai tradition, Sōtō teachers also discussed koans regularly. As already noted, Hongzhi studied briefly with Dahui's master, Yuanwu Keqin, compiler of the model koan collection, *Blue Cliff Record*. Hongzhi refers to koans in his Practice Instructions; he also compiled two noted collections of one hundred koans, one with his own verse commentaries and one with prose comments. A Chinese Sōtō master, Wansong Xingxiu

(1166–1246), later took these collections of Hongzhi's and added extensive explication, thus creating the *Book of Serenity* and *Record of Further Inquiry*. Similarly, Hongzhi's teacher Danxia Zichun had also assembled one hundred cases with his own appended verses, which became the basis for another koan anthology, the *Vacant Hall Collection*. Eihei Dōgen likewise devotes much of his masterwork *Shōbōgenzō (Treasury of the True Dharma Eye)* to commentary on the old stories.

Dahui's criticism of silent illumination relates to the differing effect of koans and sitting meditation in practice, rather than to a total rejection of one mode or the other. We know that Dahui himself remained dedicated to sitting meditation from Dōgen's praise for Dahui's determination to maintain such meditation on an occasion when he was seriously ill.[20] Dahui was also sensitive to overemphasizing koan practice above personal experience, which sometimes led to excessively intellectual, obsessive literary study of the old stories. (So great was his concern, in fact, that Dahui destroyed the printing blocks for the *Blue Cliff Record*, compiled by his own teacher. Fortunately, copies of the work survived.)[21]

With regard to silent illumination specifically, Dahui charged that its advocates "just teach people to stop and rest and play dead"; they "sit wordlessly with eyes shut beneath the black mountain . . . [and] don't seek subtle wondrous enlightenment."[22] To be sure, the misapplication and misunderstanding of silent illumination meditation sometimes has led to self-satisfied, tranquilized, uninsightful, and unresponsive practitioners. Conversely, highly systematized koan practice, predominantly a feature of the Rinzai tradition, sometimes has the tendency to encourage the student to "pass through" successive koans in a formalized program of accomplishment, rather than "becoming" the story and its teaching. In both cases a role of the teacher is to correct such deviations and to keep the practice balanced.

Dahui claims that silent illumination produces addiction to calmness by emphasizing concentration at the expense of insight. However, the teaching of Hongzhi himself, as presented in the Practice Instructions, balances these two qualities. And in his important poem "Guidepost of Silent Illumination," Hongzhi clearly stresses the indispensability and interdependence of both serenity (or calm) and illumination (or insight): "if illumination neglects serenity, then aggressiveness appears . . . if serenity neglects illumination, murkiness leads to wasted dharma" (useless teaching).

Hongzhi's teaching, though perhaps misapplied by some of his followers, encourages active functioning appropriate to the everyday phenomenal world. The balancing of serenity and illumination is analogous to the balancing of awareness of the absolute and of the relative as described in the five ranks. The ultimate purpose of spiritual practice is to realize both wisdom's illuminating insight and its appropriate functioning in the ordinary world of beings: bodhisattvic responsiveness and responsibility. Hongzhi depicts this process of meditative realization:

> The ancestral masters' nostrils and patch-robed monks' life pulse consists of holding firmly and then releasing in activity so that we all discover our own freedom. So it is said that false [thinking] is stopped and stillness [concentration] necessarily arises, stillness arises and wisdom appears, wisdom arises and stillness necessarily disappears [in active functioning]. Clear and distinct, this is the only authentic view.

For Hongzhi the whole purpose of practice is to "graciously share yourself with the hundred grass tips [i.e., myriad beings] in the busy marketplace." Hongzhi frequently exhorts his listeners to study and to embody the teaching more thoroughly and penetratingly, and to persist in going beyond their current realization. Again and again he urges us to actualize the state of total awareness.

Hongzhi's Relation to Dōgen

The influence of Hongzhi's teachings since his lifetime is not predominantly through a direct lineage of successors but in his expression of the fundamental attitudes of Zen meditation. This influence is perhaps most apparent in the development of his teachings by the Japanese Sōtō school, which derives from Dōgen and in recent decades has spread to Western countries. In this tradition Hongzhi is revered as a major forerunner, even though the Japanese Sōtō school descends not from him but from one of his dharma-brothers. Hongzhi's writings are also still greatly appreciated in Chinese Zen, although given the cooperative intermingling of schools and lineages in modern Chinese Buddhism, it is unclear whether any contemporary Chinese Zen teachers are descendants of Hongzhi.

Hongzhi's direct lineage did achieve some degree of longevity. One of his successors, Si-de Huihui, had two descendants four and five generations after him who went to Japan, Dongming Huiji (1272–1340) and Dongling Yungyu (d. 1365).[23] There they established a branch of the Sōtō tradition referred to as the Wanshi-ha (Japanese for "Hongzhi school"), which was housed mostly amid the Japanese Rinzai temples (where prowess in Chinese cultural matters was valued), and whose followers also extensively studied the five ranks teachings. This lineage survived well into the sixteenth century, but seems to have had little contact with the Sōtō branch established by Dōgen.

Because awareness of Hongzhi in contemporary Buddhist studies and practice has been dwarfed by appreciation of Dōgen, whose genius is esteemed as a unique and fresh Japanese synthesis of Buddhist teaching as it developed in the Chinese Zen tradition, it seems appropriate in tracing Hongzhi's influence on Zen to compare his teachings with those of Dōgen. Examining primary aspects of Dōgen's practice is also helpful in more fully understanding practical implementations and intentions of Hongzhi's meditation teachings, and in turn reveals the great extent of Dōgen's indebtedness to Hongzhi.

Eihei Dōgen went to China and received transmission of the Sōtō teachings in 1227 from Tiantong Rujing (1163–1228), the abbot of the same Jingde Monastery on Mount Tiantong where Hongzhi had been abbot, and a third-generation successor to Changlu Qingliao, a dharma-brother of Hongzhi (both were disciples of Danxia Zichun). Dōgen clearly reveres Hongzhi, referring to him particularly as an ancient buddha, and says that Hongzhi is also the only person Rujing ever called an "ancient buddha."[24]

Hongzhi's influence on Dōgen can be seen most clearly in their meditation practice and in their understanding of its meaning. Dōgen calls the silent illumination meditation taught by Hongzhi *shikan taza* or "just sitting," an expression for silent illumination used by Rujing. This objectless and nondualistic meditation does not involve stages or striving for any goal or achievement; thus it is an activity radically other than the usual worldly activity, which grasps and seeks for some result. Hongzhi encourages this practice when he says, "Stay with that just as that. Stay with this just as this." For Hongzhi, you already have

the shining "field of boundless emptiness . . . from the very beginning." There is no place else to look. "People who sincerely
meditate and authentically arrive trust that the field has always
been with them." Hongzhi clarifies this grounding exhaustively
through continual emphasis of wholeness and nonseparation.
Nothing is external to this luminous present mind.

Dōgen expresses the same understanding when he urges
practitioners to "have no design on becoming a buddha," since
this meditation is already "the dharma gate of repose and bliss,
the practice-realization of totally culminated enlightenment."[25]
The unity of practice and enlightenment is central to Dōgen's
teaching. While it is essential to realize fully this perfect, all-
pervasive Mind, which is no place other than right here, and is
naturally undefiled, arriving at some theoretical understanding
of this truth is not enough. It must be personally practiced, enacted, fully exerted, and celebrated.

Hongzhi likewise repeatedly urges his listeners to fully embody this teaching and experience it personally: "Even if you
thoroughly understand, still please practice until it is familiar";
Mind must actively "accord and respond without laboring and
accomplish without hindrance." For Dōgen this is embodied in
zazen (seated meditation), and also in sincere mindful conduct of
ordinary everyday life (as expressed, for example, in Zhaozhou's
"wash out your bowl" and "drink your tea," mentioned by
Hongzhi in his Practice Instructions).

One distillation of Hongzhi's meditation is his poem "The
Acupuncture Needle of Zazen" (see Religious Verses), which
Dōgen praises and compares favorably with other Zen teachers'
descriptions of meditation. He calls the latter "nothing but
models for reverting to the source and returning to the origin,
vain programs for suspending considerations and congealing in

tranquillity," unlike Hongzhi's "Needle," which "says it right. It alone radiates throughout the surface and interior of the realm of the dharma."[26]

In this poem Hongzhi speaks of "illuminating without encountering objects, . . . complete without grasping, [and] knowing without touching things, . . . never engaging in discriminating thinking." This is dynamic, radiant awareness, not the suppression of thoughts characteristic of the quietistic concentration that Dahui warned against. The Sōtō monk and scholar Menzan Zuihō (1682–1769),[27] who was instrumental in establishing contemporary Sōtō Zen understanding, comments on Hongzhi's verse:

> If you think that you have cut off illusory mind, instead of simply clarifying how illusory mind *melts* [italics mine], illusory mind will come up again, as though you had cut the stem of a blade of grass . . . and left the root alive.[28]

Hongzhi's objectless illumination does not deny the objectifications in our experience, but simply allows them to melt naturally into unified awareness.

In Dōgen's essay named after Hongzhi's poem, in which he quotes "The Acupuncture Needle of Zazen," Dōgen ends by offering his own version as an elaboration and development of Hongzhi's.[29] Dōgen's "Needle" poem amplifies Hongzhi's "illumination without encountering objects" to emphasize that completeness is itself realization and is enacted by effort without desire (themes also apparent in Hongzhi's Practice Instructions). Dōgen concludes his own poem by saying that it is not that Hongzhi "has not yet said it right, but it can also be said like this."[30]

Although this meditation does not ultimately involve concentration on an object or stages of advancement, it is not without technique. In his "Song of the Grass-Roof Hermitage," Shitou had said, "Turn around the light to shine within and then just return." In his Practice Instructions Hongzhi makes similar suggestions, urging practitioners to "take the backward step and directly reach the middle of the circle from where light issues forth," and elsewhere to "turn within and drop off everything completely, and realization will occur."

The backward step of turning the light to shine within, directing one's attention to observe closely one's own awareness, is a basic Zen meditation technique, called *ekō henshō* in Japanese. Dōgen says it is necessary to

> cease practice based on intellectual understanding, pursuing words and following after speech, and learn the backward step that turns your light inwardly to illuminate yourself. Body and mind of themselves will drop away and your original face will be manifest.[31]

Dōgen elucidates this key technique, which he refers to as "the essential art of zazen," in an essay in which he quotes a dialogue from Yaoshan Weiyen (745–828), who was the direct successor to Shitou and the teacher of Dongshan's teacher, Yunyan. A monk asked Yaoshan what he thought about when he was meditating. Yaoshan said he thought of that which doesn't think. The monk asked *how* he did that, and Yaoshan said, "Beyond-thinking."[32] In a different version of this essay, in place of this dialogue Dōgen wrote:

> Whenever a thought occurs, be aware of it, as soon as you are aware of it, it will vanish. If you remain for a long period forgetful of objects, you will naturally become unified. This is the essential art of zazen.[33]

This turning the light of attentive awareness within to see and feel the nature of one's own thinking process and the vast luminous space around and beneath these thought nodules (i.e., that which doesn't think) is a central technique of Hongzhi's meditation teaching.

If the technique of objectless meditation is to "turn your light inwardly to illuminate the self," its fulfillment occurs when "body and mind of themselves drop away and the original face is manifested." Hongzhi describes this enlightening letting go of body-mind in his Practice Instructions when he says, "The essence is to empty and open out body and mind, as expansive as the great emptiness of space. Naturally in the entire territory all is satisfied." Hongzhi also urges his students to "cast off completely your head and skin," suggesting that they "let everything entirely fall away and put it all together without any extraneous conditions. This is referred to as the occasion of solitary, glorious unselfishness."

This "dropping off of body and mind," called *shinjin datsuraku* in Japanese, is crucial to Dōgen's teaching and refers to the incident of his enlightenment at the Jingde Monastery in 1227. Dōgen was sitting in the meditation hall when his teacher, Rujing, chastised the monk next to Dōgen, who was sleeping, saying, "To study the way is to cast off body-mind. Why are you engaged in single-minded sleep instead of single-minded meditation?" It is said that Dōgen was thereupon greatly enlightened. He went to Rujing's room and said, "Body-mind is cast [or dropped] off." Rujing agreed, "Body-mind is cast off, casting off body-mind." Dōgen asked that he not be approved so easily, and Rujing replied that this was "casting off cast off."[34]

This dropping off or letting go of attachment to body-mind is the purposeful yet unlabored release of all obstructions to fundamental clear illuminated Mind. As Shitou says in the "Song of the Grass-Roof Hermitage," "Let go of hundreds of years and relax completely." In a frequently quoted passage, Dōgen says:

> Studying the Buddha Way is studying oneself. Studying oneself is forgetting oneself. Forgetting oneself is being enlightened by all things. Being enlightened by all things is causing the body-mind of oneself and the body-mind of others to be shed. There is ceasing the traces of enlightenment, which causes one to forever leave the traces of enlightenment which is cessation.[35]

The dropping off or shedding of body-mind is itself thorough realization of universal illuminating emptiness as the all-pervading nature of existence. It is understood as the highest awakening in Sōtō Zen: Menzan equates it with *anuttarasaṃyak-sambodhi*, unsurpassed perfected buddhahood.[36]

There has been speculation as to whether Dōgen's teaching of dropping off body-mind really derived from Rujing—that Dō-gen misunderstood Rujing, who was really speaking only of casting off the dusts (defilements) from the mind, and that this misunderstanding, or his intentional reinterpretation, led to Dō-gen's enlightenment and his own, original formulation of *shinjin datsuraku*. These speculations now seem dubious.[37] Certainly Dōgen fully developed and articulated the teaching of dropping body-mind beyond Rujing's usage. Yet the extent of Dōgen's connection with the understanding of his Sōtō forerunners may be elucidated by seeing how this teaching actually echoes Hong-zhi.

The sparse records of Rujing, other than those from Dōgen, reveal many suggestions that students shed the mind's dusts but not "drop off body-mind." Hongzhi's Practice Instructions, however, include frequent exhortations to drop off dusts, as well as many references (such as those mentioned above) to a more totalistic letting go that refer not to a dualistic view of sense dusts as real or external, but clearly to the same vast awareness as Dōgen's *shinjin datsuraku*.

Because this teaching is so important in Dōgen's Zen, and given contemporary questions about its derivation, a bit of linguistic comparison is called for, even in a general introduction to Hongzhi. The two characters that Dōgen uses as a compound for dropping off, *datsuraku* (in Chinese, *to lo*), individually mean to remove, and, somewhat less actively, to fall away or scatter.[38] When describing the experience of total letting go, Hongzhi frequently uses these same characters separately, *to* being combined with *jin* (exhaustively) to mean cast off completely. In one place in the Practice Instructions, however, Hongzhi does use *to* and *lo* in combination, specifically to speak of this process of letting go in meditation:

> You must completely withdraw from the invisible pounding and weaving of your ingrained ideas. If you want to be rid of this invisible [turmoil], you must just sit through it and let go of everything. Attain fulfillment and illuminate thoroughly, light and shadow altogether forgotten. *Drop off* [*to lo*—my italics] your own skin, and the sense-dusts will be fully purified, the eye readily discerning the brightness. Accept your function and be wholly satisfied.

This teaching of casting off body and mind articulated by both Hongzhi and Dōgen points to the essence of silent illumination, which is simply focusing awareness on the totality of self to return to and enact the bright shining empty field that is our own fundamental nature.

The writings of Hongzhi and Dōgen also share the use of rich poetical imagery and metaphor. Dōgen is particularly known for his artful use of language, turning conventional language patterns inside out to undo conditioned thinking and demonstrate the logic of awakening. Linguistic comparisons of Hongzhi and Dōgen may well reveal further connections, both in teaching style and practice, as they both actualize the mind "beyond-thinking."

The Empty Field of Buddha Nature

Hongzhi's Practice Instructions can be framed and even introduced in terms of the teaching of buddha nature, an approach expressed in Hongzhi's Case 67 in the *Book of Serenity*:

> The Flower Ornament Scripture says, "I now see all sentient beings everywhere fully possess the wisdom and virtues of the enlightened ones, but because of false conceptions and attachments they do not realize it."[39]

This is said to be the utterance of Shakyamuni Buddha at the time of his great enlightenment, signifying recognition of the inalienable buddha nature of all beings.

Hongzhi echoes this understanding when he says, "How amazing it is that all people have this but cannot polish it into bright clarity. In darkness unawakened, they make foolishness cover their wisdom and overflow." This insight is also the basis for the very beginning of the Practice Instructions, which can be seen as a declaration of Hongzhi's whole teaching:

> The field of boundless emptiness is what exists from the very beginning. You must purify, cure, grind down, or brush away all the tendencies you have fabricated into apparent habits. Then you can reside in the clear circle of brightness.

This awakening, or buddhahood, is not something created or achieved, it is neither nonexistent nor existent. The essential practice, as understood in the Zen tradition, is simply to wake up to this, what Hongzhi calls the empty field. "It cannot be cultivated or proven. From the beginning it is altogether complete."

Although we may realize a more or less thorough vision of the empty field, in practice we are often thrown back into conditioned habitual responses concocted previously by our limited human consciousness. This practice thus further involves closely observing our delusions and using these obstructions themselves to clarify and illuminate the fundamental field of awakening. We must practice at grinding down, curing, and brushing away the "dusts" until we can enact this awareness and allow the fundamental pervasive purity to shine. Hongzhi says:

> Empty and desireless, cold and thin, simple and genuine, this is how to strike down and fold up the remaining habits of many lives. When the stains from old habits are exhausted, the original light appears, blazing through your skull, not admitting any other matters. Vast and spacious, like sky and water merging during autumn, like snow and moon having the same color, this field is without boundary, beyond direction, magnificently one entity without edge or seam. Further, when you turn within and drop off everything completely, realization occurs.

The importance of purifying or resolving one's conditioning informs the practice that underlies Hongzhi's vision of inherent illumination; once the obscurations of conditioning are shed, free functioning is manifested. This process is reflected in the traditional Sōtō approach to koan practice, which is to see the events and conflicts of our own lives as cases to be penetrated, both in meditation practice and in consultation with a teacher. This approach, called *genjōkōan* (the koan manifesting) in Dōgen's Japanese teaching, may use the traditional koan stories, but only as they apply to our own experience.[40] Hence we may see *genjōkōan* as a technique to work through our own conditioned dusts to the original boundless field and its expression in our lives. It is an aspect of turning the light within to illuminate ourselves, and so, perhaps, allow the dropping off of body-mind.

Hongzhi also emphasizes the teaching of buddha nature in his close scrutiny of perception and discrimination, showing how we falsely estrange ourselves and objectify the phenomenal world. "Haven't you yourself established the mind that thinks up all the illusory conditions? . . . The eye cannot see itself but neither can [its function] be dimmed." The importance of this investigation is indicated by Hongzhi thus:

> We all have the clear, wondrously bright field from the beginning.
> Many lifetimes of misunderstanding come only from distrust,
> hindrance, and screens of confusion that we create in a scenario
> of isolation.

The detailed analysis of the discriminating consciousness, seeing through it to return to the fundamental clear Mind, is stressed by the traditional Yogācāra branch of Buddhist teaching.[41] This practice is indicated in Shitou's "Merging of Difference and Unity":

> Each sense and every field
> Interact and do not interact;
> When interacting they also merge—
> Otherwise they remain in their own states. . . .
> Eye and form, ear and sound;
> Nose and smell, tongue and taste—

Thus in all things
The leaves spread from the root;
The whole process must return to the source.[42]

In Hongzhi's teaching of ultimate nondualistic illumination,
even these illusory screens of ignorance which we ourselves create are not outside the field of buddha nature. It may feel to us as
if the release from suffering must involve immeasurable effort
and hard work. But from the point of view of awakened mind
which Hongzhi expresses, all the hindrances in our lives are
themselves simply the manifestations of the luminous field of
truth, which we have the opportunity to illuminate and shed in
ongoing awakening:

> Directly arriving here you will be able to recognize the mind
> ground dharma field that is the root source of the ten thousand
> forms germinating with unwithered fertility. These flowers and
> leaves are the whole world. So we are told that a single seed is an
> uncultivated field. Do not weed out the new shoots, and the self
> will flower.

Hongzhi encourages our self-reliant and indestructible inherent understanding. He offers abundant examples, through images from the natural world around us, of our innate familiarity
with the workings of clear awareness and of the ease and simplicity of its expression:

> People of the Way journey through the world responding to con-
> ditions, carefree and without restraint. Like clouds finally rain-
> ing, like moonlight following the current, like orchids growing in
> shade, like spring arising in everything, they act without mind,
> they respond with certainty.

Hongzhi's use of nature metaphors to express the simple, un-affected functioning of the awakened buddha nature also reflects the Huayen teaching of the total interconnectedness and inter-dependence of all being as the realm of buddha nature:

> The white clouds are fascinated with the green mountain's foun-dation. The bright moon cherishes being carried along with the flowing water. The clouds part and the mountain appears. The moon sets and the water is cool.

Hongzhi's teaching presages such modern philosophical movements as Deep Ecology, with its sense of identity of self and ecosystem.[43] It is not just that Hongzhi uses the clouds and mountains as *metaphors* for awakened activity: the clouds ac-tually are us and the mountains are us, and also the fascination is us. We are the flowing water; we are the bright moon.

The Practice Instructions text derives from dharma talks ad-dressed to monks and laypeople, practitioners who often were al-ready fairly adept meditators. "Dharma" (a Sanskrit word) re-fers to the teaching of spiritual realization or awareness of reality, to the actual truth or reality itself, and, as "dharmas," to the par-ticular elements of the field of reality. The fulfillment of the pur-pose of such teaching, its liberative efficacy, depends largely on the awakened presence of the teacher, which is conveyed by rhythm and feeling tone as much as by literal meaning.

Hongzhi's meditation instructions describe, and evoke, the ac-tual experience of enlightened, illuminating awareness. I hope that this translation retains Hongzhi's direct simplicity, with suf-ficient annotation to elucidate references to traditional Buddhist teaching and Zen metaphor and imagery, but keeping intact the experiential and evocative quality of the original. As Dongshan puts it, "The meaning is not in the words."[44] Hongzhi wants each of us actually to experience and embody for ourselves the vast empty shining field from which we have never been separate. "If you embody it in this way, how could it not be beneficial?"

Taigen Dan Leighton

CULTIVATING THE
EMPTY FIELD

PRACTICE
INSTRUCTIONS

—

Dharma Words of Monk Hongzhi Zhengjue
of Mount Tiantong in Ming Province,
Compiled with a Preface by Monk Puqung[1]

Hongzhi made vast and empty the bright mirror and saw through it and reflected without neglect.[2] He manifested the mysterious pivot of subtle change, then trusted his fortune and certainly found the core. Only one who had the true eye and deep flowing eloquence could have mastered this! My teacher lived below Taipai Peak.[3] Dragons and elephants tromped around.[4] The hammer and chisel [of the teaching] chipped away. The meaning of his words spread widely but still conveyed the essence. Sometimes scholars and laypeople who trusted the Way asked for his directions; sometimes mendicant monks requested his instructions. They spread out paper and wrote down his responses. He spoke up and answered their questions, producing appropriate dharma talks. I have selected a few of these and arranged them in order. Ah, the emptiness of the great blue sky, the flowing of the vast ocean. I have not yet attained these utmost depths, so please excuse my attempt to record his talks. I must await the ones who mysteriously accord with spiritual awakening to pound out the rhythm of his words and appreciate their tones.

The Bright, Boundless Field

The field of boundless emptiness is what exists from the very beginning. You must purify, cure, grind down, or brush away all the tendencies you have fabricated into apparent habits. Then you can reside in the clear circle of brightness. Utter emptiness has no image, upright independence does not rely on anything. Just expand and illuminate the original truth unconcerned by external conditions. Accordingly we are told to realize that not a single thing exists. In this field birth and death do not appear. The deep source, transparent down to the bottom, can radiantly shine and can respond unencumbered to each speck of dust without becoming its partner. The subtlety of seeing and hearing transcends mere colors and sounds. The whole affair functions without leaving traces, and mirrors without obscurations. Very naturally mind and dharmas emerge and harmonize.[5] An Ancient said that non-mind embodies and fulfills the way of non-mind. Embodying and fulfilling the way of non-mind, finally you can rest. Proceeding you are able to guide the assembly. With thoughts clear, sitting silently, wander into the center of the circle of wonder. This is how you must penetrate and study.

The Practice of True Reality

The practice of true reality is simply to sit serenely in silent introspection. When you have fathomed this you cannot be turned around by external causes and conditions. This empty, wide open mind is subtly and correctly illuminating. Spacious and content, without confusion from inner thoughts of grasping, effectively overcome habitual behavior and realize the self that is not possessed by emotions. You must be broad-minded, whole without relying on others. Such upright independent spirit can begin not to pursue degrading situations. Here you can rest and become clean, pure, and lucid. Bright and penetrating, you can immediately return, accord, and respond to deal with events. Everything is unhindered, clouds gracefully floating up to the peaks, the moonlight glitteringly flowing down mountain streams.[6] The entire place is brightly illumined and spiritually transformed, totally unobstructed and clearly manifesting responsive interaction like box and cover or arrowpoints [meeting].[7] Continuing, cultivate and nourish yourself to embody maturity and achieve stability. If you accord everywhere with thorough clarity and cut off sharp corners without dependence on doctrines, like the white ox or wildcat [helping to arouse wonder], you can be called a complete person.[8] So we hear that this is how one on the way of non-mind acts, but before realizing nonmind we still have great hardship.

Face Everything, Let Go, and Attain Stability

Vast and far-reaching without boundary, secluded and pure, manifesting light, this spirit is without obstruction. Its brightness does not shine out but can be called empty and inherently radiant. Its brightness, inherently purifying, transcends causal conditions beyond subject and object. Subtle but preserved, illumined and vast, also it cannot be spoken of as being or nonbeing, or discussed with images or calculations. Right in here the central pivot turns, the gateway opens. You accord and respond without laboring and accomplish without hindrance. Every-

5

meditation

where turn around freely, not following conditions, not falling into classifications. Facing everything, let go and attain stability. Stay with that just as that. Stay with this just as this. That and this are mixed together with no discriminations as to their places. So it is said that the earth lifts up the mountain without knowing the mountain's stark steepness; a rock contains jade without knowing the jade's flawlessness. This is how truly to leave home, how home-leaving must be embodied.[9]

Contemplating the Ten Thousand Years

Patch-robed monks make their thinking dry and cool and rest from the remnants of conditioning.[10] Persistently brush up and sharpen this bit of the field. Directly cut through all the overgrown grass. Reach the limit in all directions without defiling even one atom. Spiritual and bright, vast and lustrous, illuminating fully what is before you, directly attain the shining light and clarity that cannot attach to a single defilement. Immediately tug and pull back the ox's nose.[11] Of course his horns are imposing and he stomps around like a beast, yet he never damages people's sprouts or grain. Wandering around, accept how it goes. Accepting how it goes, wander around. Do not be bounded by or settle into any place. Then the plough will break open the ground in the field of the empty *kalpa*.[12] Proceeding in this manner, each event will be unobscured, each realm will appear complete. One contemplation of the ten thousand years is beginning not to dwell in appearances. Thus it is said that the mind-ground contains every seed, and the universal rain makes them all sprout. When awakening blossoms, desires fade, and Bodhi's fruit is perfected self.[13]

Performing the Buddha Work

[The empty field] cannot be cultivated or proven. From the beginning it is altogether complete, undefiled and clear down to the bottom. Where everything is correct and totally sufficient, attain the pure eye that illuminates thoroughly, fulfilling liberation. Enlightenment involves embodying this; stability develops from practicing it. Birth and death originally have no root or stem, appearing and disappearing originally have no defining signs or traces. The primal light, empty and effective, illumines the head-top. The primal wisdom, silent but also glorious, responds to conditions. When you reach the truth without middle or edge, cutting off before and after, then you realize one wholeness. Everywhere sense faculties and objects both just happen. The one who sticks out his broad long tongue transmits the inexhaustible lamp, radiates the great light, and performs the great buddha work, from the first not borrowing from others one atom from outside the dharma.[14] Clearly this affair occurs within your own house.

Forgetting about Merit Is Fulfillment

Separate yourself from disturbance and face whatever appears before you. Not one iota seeps through from outside. The two forms [yin and yang][15] have the same root, and the ten thousand images have one substance. Following change and going along with transformation, the whole is not clouded over by previous conditions. Then you reach the foundation of the great freedom. Wind blows and moon shines, and beings do not obstruct each other. Afterwards, settle back within and take responsibility. Wisdom returns and the principle is consummated. When you forget about merit your position is fulfilled. Do not fall for occupying honorable stations, but enter the current of the world and join with the delusion. Transcendent, solitary, and glorious, directly know that transmitting is merit, but having transmitted is not your own merit.

The Ground That Sages Cannot Transmit

Cast off completely your head and skin. Thoroughly withdraw from distinctions of light and shadow. Where the ten thousand changes do not reach is the foundation that even a thousand sages cannot transmit. Simply by yourself illuminate and deeply experience it with intimate accord. The original light flashes through confusion. True illumination reflects into the distance. Deliberations about being and nonbeing are entirely abandoned. The wonder appears before you, its benefit transferred out for *kalpas*. Immediately you follow conditions and accord with awakening without obstruction from any defilements. The mind does not attach to things, and your footsteps are not visible on the road. Then you are called to continue the family business.[16] Even if you thoroughly understand, still please practice until it is familiar.

With Total Trust Roam and Play in Samādhi

Empty and desireless, cold and thin, simple and genuine, this is how to strike down and fold up the remaining habits of many lives. When the stains from old habits are exhausted, the original light appears, blazing through your skull, not admitting any other matters. Vast and spacious, like sky and water merging during autumn, like snow and moon having the same color, this field is without boundary, beyond direction, magnificently one entity without edge or seam. Further, when you turn within and drop off everything completely, realization occurs. Right at the time of entirely dropping off, deliberation and discussion are one thousand or ten thousand miles away. Still no principle is discernible, so what could there be to point to or explain? People with the bottom of the bucket fallen out immediately find total trust.[17] So we are told simply to realize mutual response and explore mutual response, then turn around and enter the world. Roam and play in *samādhi*.[18] Every detail clearly appears before you. Sound and form, echo and shadow, happen instantly without leaving traces. The outside and myself do not dominate each other, only because no perceiving [of objects] comes between us. Only this nonperceiving encloses the empty space of the dharma realm's majestic ten thousand forms.[19] People with the original face should embody and fully investigate [the field] without neglecting a single fragment.

The Valley Spirit and the Wind Master

Patch-robed monks practice thoroughly without carrying a single thread. Open-mindedly sparkling and pure, they are like a mirror reflecting a mirror, with nothing regarded as outside, without capacity for accumulating dust. They illuminate everything fully, perceiving nothing [as an object]. This is called taking up the burden from inside and is how to shoulder responsibility. Wisdom illuminates the darkness without confusion. The Way integrates with the body and does not get stuck. From this unstuck place, engaging and transforming at the appropriate opportunity, the wisdom does not leak out. Clearly the Way does not get stained. The valley spirit echoes the sound.[20] The wind master walks in the sky. Unobstructed and free, beyond restraints, they do not depend on even subtle indicators, and their essential spirit cannot be eclipsed. Fulfilled, wander around and arrive at such a field. The entire place secure, the entire place at leisure, the open field of the white ox is plain and simple, of one color. If you chase the ox, still he will not go away. You must intimately experience and arrive here.

Simply Drop Off Everything

Silently dwell in the self, in true suchness abandon conditioning. Open-minded and bright without defilement, simply penetrate and drop off everything. Today is not your first arrival here. Since the ancient home before the empty *kalpa*, clearly nothing has been obscured. Although you are inherently spirited and splendid, still you must go ahead and enact it. When doing so, immediately display every atom without hiding a speck of dirt. Dry and cool in deep repose, profoundly understand. If your rest is not satisfying and you yearn to go beyond birth and death, there can be no such place. Just burst through and you will discern without thought-dusts, pure without reasons for anxiety. Stepping back with open hands, [giving up everything], is thoroughly comprehending life and death. Immediately you can sparkle and respond to the world. Merge together with all things. Everywhere is just right. Accordingly we are told that from ancient to modern times all dharmas are not concealed, always apparent and exposed.

The Ancient Ferryboat in Bright Moonlight

A patch-robed monk's authentic task is to practice the essence, in each minute event carefully discerning the shining source, radiant without discrimination, one color unstained. You must keep turning inward, then [the source] is apprehended. This is called being able to continue the family business. Do not wear the changing fashions, transcend the duality of light and shadow. Accordingly the ancestors' single trail is marvelously embodied.[21] The residual debris of the world departs, its influence ended. This worldly knowledge does not compare to returning to the primary and obtaining confirmation. Observing beyond your skull, the core finally can be fulfilled and you can emerge from the transitory. The reeds blossom under the bright moon; the ancient ferryboat begins its passage; the jade thread fits into the golden needle. Then the opportunity arises to turn around, enter the world, and respond to conditions. All the dusts are entirely yours; all the dharmas are not someone else's. Follow the current and paddle along, naturally unobstructed!

The Gates Sparkling at the Source

All buddhas and every ancestor without exception testify that they all arrive at this refuge where the three times [past, present, and future] cease and the ten thousand changes are silenced. Straight ahead, unopposed by the smallest atom, the inherently illumined buddha spirit subtly penetrates the original source. When recognized and realized exhaustively, [this spirit] shares itself and responds to situations. The gates sparkle and all beings behold the gleaming. Then they understand that from within this place fulfilled self flows out. The hundreds of grass tips all around never are imposed as my causes and conditioning. The whole body from head to foot proceeds smoothly.

The Misunderstanding of Many Lifetimes

Emptiness is without characteristics. Illumination has no emotional afflictions. With piercing, quietly profound radiance, it mysteriously eliminates all disgrace. Thus one can know oneself; thus the self is completed. We all have the clear, wondrously bright field from the beginning. Many lifetimes of misunderstanding come only from distrust, hindrance, and screens of confusion that we create in a scenario of isolation. With boundless wisdom journey beyond this, forgetting accomplishments. Straightforwardly abandon stratagems and take on responsibility. Having turned yourself around, accepting your situation, if you set foot on the path, spiritual energy will marvelously transport you. Contact phenomena with total sincerity, not a single atom of dust outside yourself.

Self and Other the Same

All dharmas are innately amazing beyond description. Perfect vision has no gap. In mountain groves, grasslands, and woods the truth has always been exhibited. Discern and comprehend the broad long tongue [of Buddha's teaching], which cannot be muted anywhere. The spoken is instantly heard; what is heard is instantly spoken. Senses and objects merge; principle and wisdom are united. When self and other are the same, mind and dharmas are one. When you face what you have excluded and see how it appears, you must quickly gather it together and integrate with it. Make it work within your house, then establish stable sitting.

Ten Billion Illuminating Spirits

The Way wanders in the empty middle of the circle, reaching the vacancy where appearances are forgotten. The pure ultimate self blazes, brilliant simply from inherent illumination. Facing the boundary of the object world without yet creating the sense gates, realize the subtlety of how to eliminate the effects of the swirling flow of arising and extinction! Rely only on the source of creation. If you feel a shadow of a hair's gap, nothing will be received.[22] Just experience and respond appropriately. From this singular impact many thousands of roads open, and all things are preeminent. With this unification I radiantly speak the dharma. The self divides into ten billion distinct illuminating spirits. Distinguish these without falling into names and classifications and accord fully without effort. The mirror is clear and magnanimous. The valley is empty, but echoes. From the beginning unbound by seeing or hearing, the genuine self romps and plays in *samādhi* without obstruction. When embodied like this, how could it not be beneficial?

Sit Empty of Worldly Anxiety

If you truly appreciate a single thread your eye can suitably meet the world and its changes. Seeing clearly, do not be fooled, and the ten thousand situations cannot shroud you. Moonlight falls on the water; wind blows over the pines. Light and shadow do not confuse us; sounds or voices do not block us. The whistling wind can resonate, pervading without impediment through the various structures. Flowing along with things, harmonizing without deviation, thoroughly abandoning webs of dust, still one does not yet arrive in the original home. Put to rest the remnants of your conditioning. Sit empty of worldly anxiety, silent and bright, clear and illuminating, blank and accepting, far-reaching and responsive. Without encountering external dusts, fulfilled in your own spirit, arrive at this field and immediately recognize your ancestors.

How to Contemplate Buddha

Contemplating your own authentic form is how to contemplate Buddha. If you can experience yourself without distractions, simply surpass partiality and go beyond conceptualizing. All buddhas and all minds reach the essential without duality. Patch-robed monks silently wander and tranquilly dwell in the empty spirit, wondrously penetrating, just as the supreme emptiness permeates this dusty *kalpa*. Dignified without relying on others and radiant beyond doubt, maintaining this as primary, the energy turns around and transforms all estrangement. Passing through the world responding to situations, illumination is without striving and functions without leaving traces. From the beginning the clouds leisurely release their rain, drifting past obstacles. The direct teaching is very pure and steady. Nothing can budge it. Immediately, without allowing past conditions to turn you, genuinely embody it.

Return to the Source and Serve the Ancestors

Those who produce descendants are called ancestors. Where the stream emerges is called the source. After beholding the source and recognizing the ancestors, before your awareness can disperse, be steadfast and do not follow birth and death or past conditioning. If you do not succumb, then all beings will show the whole picture. Wake up, and in turn the ground, the roots, and the dusts are clearly cast off.[23] Although empty of desires, with deliberations cut off, transcendent comprehension is not all sealed up. Perfect bright understanding is carefree amid ten thousand images and cannot be confused. Within each dust mote is vast abundance. In a hundred thousand *samādhis* all gates are majestic, all dharmas are fulfilled. Still you must gather them together and bring them within. To reach the time-honored, return to the source and serve the ancestors. Joined together into unity, scrutinize yourself and go on.

The Whole Arrives in Original Brightness

The place of silent and serene illumination is the heavenly dome in clear autumn, shining brightly without strain, gleaming through both light and shadow. At this juncture the whole is supreme and genuinely arrives. The clear source is embodied with spirit, the axis is wide and the energy lively, everything apparent in the original brightness. The center is manifest and is celebrated. All the various events are consummated, with yin and yang balanced and the ten thousand representations equalized. Smooth and level, magnificently peaceful, from north to south, from east to west, heaven is the same as heaven, people are the same as people, responsive with their bodies, visible in their forms, speaking the dharma. This ability is fully actualized, extensively obliterating obstacles.

Spectacular Images of Clouds and Dragons

In the wind abode clouds and dragons harmoniously follow each other.[24] Very naturally from the first they do not [need to] express their intentions to each other. Similarly, patch-robed monks are accommodating and, based on causes and conditions, can harmoniously practice together. Arriving without display, emerging unconcealed, the wondrous [clouds and dragons] enter the whole scene and cannot be confused. Casually hanging above the ten thousand features, each distinctly presents a spectacular image. Complete without a hair's difference between them, springing forth with spontaneity, they clearly exemplify coming home, but still must investigate until they have eaten their fill. Clouds disperse and winds die down. The autumn sky clears and the moon sets. The waters of heaven are limitless. Where the ground is on its own, the brightness begins to be realized.

Buddha Flowers, Leaves, Roots, and Dusts

The Way is not what the ancestors transmit. Before the ancestors come, it already pervades the whole environment. Emptiness is inherently without characteristics; spirituality cannot be imitated. On its own, illumination emerges from causes and conditions. Constantly living apart from surface appearances is called being the ancestor. Simply certify and unite with it; you cannot be handed it. All buddhas arrive here and regard this as the ultimate. They respond to transformations and disperse their bodies as flowers, leaves, roots, and dusts. Wisdom enters the three times, and the ten thousand changes do not disturb us, each dust is not outside us. This marvel is beyond the vast thousands of classical texts, so where could you hold on to the shadowy world?

The Backward Step and the Upright Cauldron

With the depths clear, utterly silent, thoroughly illuminate the source, empty and spirited, vast and bright. Even though you have lucidly scrutinized your image and no shadow or echo meets it, searching throughout you see that you still have distinguished between the merits of a hundred undertakings. Then you must take the backward step and directly reach the middle of the circle from where light issues forth.[25] Outstanding and independent, still you must abandon pretexts for merit. Carefully discern that naming engenders beings and that these rise and fall with intricacy. When you can share your self, then you may manage affairs, and you have the pure seal that stamps the ten thousand forms. Traveling the world, meeting conditions, the self joyfully enters *samādhi* in all delusions and accepts its function, which is to empty out the self so as not to be full of itself.[26] The empty valley receives the clouds. The cold stream cleanses the moon. Not departing and not remaining, far beyond all the changes, you can give teachings without attainment or expectation. Everything everywhere comes back to the olden ground. Not a hair has been shifted, bent, or raised up. Despite a hundred uglinesses or a thousand stupidities, the upright cauldron is naturally beneficent.[27] Zhaozhou's answers "wash out your bowl" and "drink your tea" do not require making arrangements; from the beginning they have always been perfectly apparent.[28] Thoroughly observing each thing with the whole eye is a patch-robed monk's spontaneous conduct.

Beaming through All Gloom

Study the Buddha and research his lineage's subtlety. You must clarify your heart, dive into the spirit, and silently wander in contemplation, apprehending the dharma's source. Without pettiness, or weaving hairs to create an obstacle, be magnanimous beyond appearances. Splendid and lustrous like the waters moistening autumn, noble like the moon overwhelming the darkness, from the beginning just beam through all gloom, profoundly free from stain. Constantly still and constantly glorious, the stillness is not extinguished by causes, the glory is not marred by shadows. Vacant, round, and pure, the empty *kalpa* will not shift, shake, or obscure [this source]. Able to be serene, and able to know, here you can walk securely. The jade vessel turns over on its side, at once dispensing energy for you to return, share yourself, and respond to the world. In this realm are the separate, limited forms, but all are only what the self establishes, arising along with our own four elements.[29] How could there be an obstruction? Since [this mind] is entirely without obstruction, there is no difference between that one and me, self and other are not separated by their names. Sounds and colors crowd in together, carefree and transcendent, directly leaping into each other. So it is said that mountains and rivers are not separated. You should embody this like the brightness apparent everywhere.

The Mind Ground Dharma Field and the Single Seed

The field of bright spirit is an ancient wilderness that does not change. With boundless eagerness wander around this immaculate wide plain. The drifting clouds embrace the mountain; the family wind is relaxed and simple.[30] The autumn waters display the moon in its pure brightness. Directly arriving here you will be able to recognize the mind ground dharma field that is the root source of the ten thousand forms germinating with unwithered fertility. These flowers and leaves are the whole world. So we are told that a single seed is an uncultivated field. Do not weed out the new shoots, and the self will flower.

The Clouds' Fascination and the Moon's Cherishing

A person of the Way fundamentally does not dwell anywhere. The white clouds are fascinated with the green mountain's foundation. The bright moon cherishes being carried along with the flowing water. The clouds part and the mountain appears. The moon sets and the water is cool. Each bit of autumn contains vast interpenetration without bounds. Every dust is whole without reaching me; the ten thousand changes are stilled without shaking me. If you can sit here with stability, then you can freely step across and engage the world with energy. There is an excellent saying that the six sense doors are not veiled, the highways in all directions have no footprints. Always arriving everywhere without being confused, gentle without hesitation, the perfected person knows where to go.

Breezing through the World

Vast space is all-embracing, the same as ultimate emptiness. Developed skill is equally effective for all the ten thousand forms. If not a single dust is distinguished outside, then you can adapt to changing circumstances. If not one speck is left over inside, then immediately you can abide in meditation. Since the inside is empty and can respond, absorbing or not absorbing is equal. Since the outside is interconnected and constantly vacant, abiding or not abiding is all the same. Patch-robed monks enter *samādhi* just like their home wind that breezes through the entire world.

The Wonder Verified and Fulfilled

The dharma realm in the ten directions arises from the single mind. When the single mind is still, all appearances are entirely exhausted. Which one is over there? Which one is myself? Only when you do not differentiate forms, suddenly not a single dust is established, not a single recollection is produced. Discern that even before the pregnant womb and after your skin bag, each moment is astonishing radiance, full and round without direction or corners, discarding trifles. Where truly nothing can be obscured is called self-knowledge. Only thus knowing the self is called original realization, not even a hair received undeservingly. Magnificent, subtly maintaining uniqueness, genuine hearing is without sound. So it is said that perceiving without eye or ear is where the wonder is verified and fulfilled. Light streams forth from there and many thousands of images appear. Every being is actually it, altogether in the realm where patch-robed monks function on their own. It is essential only not to borrow from other people's homes. To cultivate our house you must clearly and intimately experience it for yourself.

All Beings Are Your Ancestors

Fully appreciate the emptiness of all dharmas. Then all minds are free and all dusts evaporate in the original brilliance shining everywhere. Transforming according to circumstances, meet all beings as your ancestors. Subtly illuminate all conditions, magnanimous beyond all duality. Clear and desireless, the wind in the pines and the moon in the water are content in their elements. Without minds interacting, [wind and pines or moon and water] do not impede one another. Essentially you exist inside emptiness and have the capacity to respond outwardly without being annoyed, like spring blossoming, like a mirror reflecting forms. Amid all the noise spontaneously emerge transcendent.

Rolling and Unrolling

Where the field is secure and familiar, when the great work is like a clear, cool pond, then you will see the empty *kalpa*. Do not allow a hair to bind you or permit a fiber to screen you. Be supremely empty and bright, pure, round, and glorious. The ten thousand ancients appear in succession, undisguised. If you know the whole story with a nod of your head, you will not chase after birth and death and will not dwell in nihilism or eternalism. If you want to make appropriate changes, then you must transform majestically along with the ten thousand forms. If you want to be still and abiding, you must accord with the process of containing and covering like earth and heaven (yin and yang).[31] Appearing or disappearing and rolling or unrolling are entirely up to you. In this way, people with the original face must know how to gather together or release.

Drop Off Your Skin, Accept Your Function

In daytime the sun, at night the moon, each in turn does not blind the other. This is how a patch-robed monk steadily practices, naturally without edges or seams. To gain such steadiness you must completely withdraw from the invisible pounding and weaving of your ingrained ideas. If you want to be rid of this invisible [turmoil], you must just sit through it and let go of everything. Attain fulfillment and illuminate thoroughly, light and shadow altogether forgotten.[32] Drop off your own skin, and the sense-dusts will be fully purified, the eye readily discerning the brightness. Accept your function and be wholly satisfied. In the entire place you are not restricted; the whole time you still mutually respond.

Right in light there is darkness; right in darkness there is light.[33]
A solitary boat carries the moon; at night it lodges amid the reed
flowers, gently swaying in total brilliance.

Everyone Included in the Field

Immaculate and dazzling, [the field's] limits cannot be seen with
the eyes' strength. Serene and expansive, its directions and corners cannot be found with the mind's conditioning. People who
sincerely meditate and authentically arrive trust that the field has
always been with them. Buddhas and demons cannot invade it,
pollution cannot poison it. Square or round, they just enjoy the
center. Their conduct and practice accord with the standard.
With amazing effectiveness, as numerous as grains of sand in the
River Ganges, they harmoniously mature each other.[34] From this
field our life arises; from this field it is fulfilled. This matter includes everybody. Just go forward for me and try to see. People
who know its truth nod their heads with comprehension.

The Third Eye and Bent Elbow

With the forearm bending back to meet [the body] one can respond to every event. The third eye by itself illuminates the solitary casting off of the body.[35] Both of these gather in or release
with no inside or outside. Many thousands of realms emerge
equally with oneself; the three times are naturally transcended.
Vast emptiness is boundless, genuinely illuminated by its own
brightness. This is when the illusory appearances are all exhausted. What is not exhausted is the profound spirit, absolute
beyond life and death. Arrive at this field, openly letting go of de-

pendency. When conditioned dusts do not pollute it, all situations are intimately matched. Box and cover [joining] and arrow-points [meeting] are auspicious and do not miss the mark. Roaming and playing in *samādhi*, people in this state accept their function. This upper eye and completely bent elbow are the sole matter that this monk transmits and that you should thoroughly embody.

Beyond the Various Kinds

Receive correctly this monk's word-stream, neither frozen nor trickling away, neither transparent nor muddy. When you wring it dry, take advantage of the opportunity; when you enter the bustle, perceive with your whole eye. Thorough understanding and the changing world fulfill each other totally without obstacle. The moon accompanies the current, the wind bends the grass. They sparkle and sway. After all one is not confused. So it is said that the various kinds are not equal, but beyond each of them is the path. Responding to this occasion you may proceed accordingly. Above the white grass tips, take what you have gathered and bring it back and so act appropriately.[36] Find your seat, wear your robe, and go forward and see for yourself.

Noninterference in the Matter of Oneness

The matter of oneness cannot be learned at all. The essence is to empty and open out body and mind, as expansive as the great emptiness of space. Naturally in the entire territory all is satisfied. This strong spirit cannot be deterred; in event after event it cannot be confused. The moon accompanies the flowing water, the rain pursues the drifting clouds. Settled, without a [grasping] mind, such intensity may be accomplished. Only do not let yourself interfere with things, and certainly nothing will interfere with you. Body and mind are one suchness; outside this body there is nothing else. The same substance and the same function, one nature and one form, all faculties and all object-dusts are instantly transcendent. So it is said, the sage is without self and yet nothing is not himself.[37] Whatever appears is instantly understood, and you know how to gather it up or how to let it go. Be a white ox in the open field. Whatever happens, nothing can drive him away.

The Conduct of the Moon and Clouds

The consistent conduct of people of the Way is like the flowing clouds with no [grasping] mind, like the full moon reflecting universally, not confined anywhere, glistening within each of the ten thousand forms. Dignified and upright, emerge and make contact with the variety of phenomena, unstained and unconfused. Function the same toward all others since all have the same substance as you. Language cannot transmit [this conduct], speculation cannot reach it. Leaping beyond the infinite and cutting off the dependent, be obliging without looking for merit. This marvel cannot be measured with consciousness or emotion. On the journey accept your function, in your house please sustain it. Comprehending birth and death, leaving causes and conditions, genuinely realize that from the outset your spirit is not halted. So we have been told that the mind that embraces all the ten directions does not stop anywhere.

The Resting of the Streams and Tides

Just resting is like the great ocean accepting hundreds of streams, all absorbed into one flavor. Freely going ahead is like the great surging tides riding on the wind, all coming onto this shore together. How could they not reach into the genuine source? How could they not realize the great function that appears before us? A patch-robed monk follows movement and responds to changes in total harmony. Moreover, haven't you yourself established the mind that thinks up all the illusory conditions? This insight must be perfectly incorporated.

Thirty Years of Emptiness and Existence

Authentic clarity is without blemishes. The five degrees of achievement are finally consummated.[38] At this time of not discriminating, instantly there is the whole body. The eye cannot see itself, but neither can its function be dimmed. The light streams out from the source, pure and white, shining everywhere. The reed flowers intermingle with the snow; the bright moon bathes the autumn. Here you have the energetic opportunity for mutual union.[39] On the path of careful observation, valiantly carry it and apply it well. No place can be other than myself; no place can restrain me. Leap out supreme from the ten thousand forms. Juzhi's one-finger Zen is not exhausted by thirty years of using it.[40] Its subtlety is in its simplicity, which silently, wordlessly secures the purpose at its leisure. Therefore it responds without clutching at things. The Way wanders with the spirits protecting it. This is how the principle is originally. But if suddenly you attach to one thread or fiber, then the guiding mind is obstructed and cannot get through, the gateway is blocked and cannot be opened. Where emptiness is empty it contains all of existence, where existence exists it joins the single emptiness. Still I ask, what is this?

Turning the Pearl

The original source empties out, without representation. When moved it can respond. Then you must peer right through it. Standing solitary like a steep cliff, wide open and accessible, spirited and independent, clear and bright, all this does not even slightly involve external conditions. Such activity is called the single bright occasion, which arrives right along with the ten thousand forms that emerge and are extinguished. The realm where the *samādhi* of all dusts arises [entering all *samādhis* through one *samādhi*] is clear like the ocean seal.[41] Turn it around as if turning a pearl.[42] Let everything entirely fall away, and put it all together without any extraneous conditions. This is referred to as the occasion of solitary, glorious unselfishness. At night the moon rises and the waters glisten, the spring wind blows and the flowers blossom. With no need for meritorious activity, all is naturally perfect. Causes, conditions, fruits, and retributions, none is discerned as external. Furthermore, you must know that both the light and the circumstances have altogether vanished. Again, what is it?

A Monk's Inheritance and the Vanishing Clouds

This rustic monk's home wind is using a single begging bowl for a livelihood and regarding the ten thousand forms of the world as his inheritance.[43] Subject and object can be like images in a mirror and the moon in water, blended together with nothing left out. First, do not establish your own identity, then beings will not impose their own conditions. Each form has no form. Only in this wholeness are things not isolated. In this manner perfection is fully practiced. Given the loom of energetic opportunity the shuttle can make its passage.[44] Arriving beyond images the sense-dusts all disappear. Even then you must take the backward step and return home to scrutinize this directly in meditation until you are satisfied. The clouds vanish into a single color. The snow covers the thousand mountains. Penetrating vision brings the opening to view the total body.

The Original Dwelling

A person practicing the Way subtly goes beyond words and thoughts. Instantly authentic, one is on the affirmed path and does not attach to reasoning. Extensively intermingled, the moon flows in all the waters, the wind blows through the supreme emptiness, naturally without touching or obstructing things. Transcendent illumination and function are only illuminating without stains and functioning without leaving traces. Then you can enter *samādhi* in every sense-dust and gather the ten thousand forms in the single seal. Discontinue leaks and do not act on them.[45] This is called understanding the affair of patch-robed monks. Moreover, you must remember and return to the homeward path. The clouds evaporate in the cold sky. The autumn has departed and the mountain is barren. This is where we originally dwell.

A Ploughman on the Shining Field

From the outset patch-robed monks have this field that is a clean, spacious, broad plain. Gazing ahead beyond any precipitous barriers, within the field they plough the clouds and sow the moon. With clear bright understanding, vast and expansive, the true self accepts its function, whether emerging or disintegrating, whether in a position of receiving or releasing. Directly perform the same workings as earth and heaven (yin and yang), arising and dispersing along with the ten thousand forms. Lofty and majestic, where do they come from? Still in solitude, where do they go? So we are told that the empty sky cannot encompass it, the great earth cannot uphold it. Subtly existing beyond shapes, perfectly empty beyond names, the merit of being and nonbeing is exhausted; the paths of the worldly and the sages are transcended. Then you have the opportunity to go home. Just then, what do you know? For one hundred fifty thousand acres you can see the cold, pure, shining snow. Observing this well one can be a strong ploughman.

Nāga *Meditation*

Being withered and cold in body and mind cleanses and sharpens the field. The dusts are jumbled and then distilled, leaving each realm vacant and bright. The moon in the water reflects the light in the clearing sky. The clouds embrace the mountain with its autumn colors. Whether jet black or lush green, the profound depths have great spirit. The inherently illuminated original root is not constrained by the branches and leaves. This is the time and place to leap beyond the ten thousand emotional entanglements of innumerable *kalpas*. One contemplation of ten thousand years finally goes beyond all the transitory, and you emerge with spontaneity. The clouds traveling in the vacant valley are free, whether moving or tranquil. Agreeably enter every sense-dust, while constantly staying in *samādhi*. Therefore we have been told that *nāgas* are always in meditation, never apart from this sublime state.[46]

Investigating Wonder

In clarity the wonder exists, with spiritual energy shining on its own. It cannot be grasped and so cannot be called being. It cannot be rubbed away and so cannot be called nonbeing. Beyond the mind of deliberation and discussion, depart from the remains of the shadowy images. Emptying [one's sense of] self-existence is wondrous. This wonder is embodied with a spirit that can be reenacted. The moon mind with its cloud body is revealed straightforwardly in every direction without resorting to signs or symbols. Radiating light everywhere, it responds appropriately to beings and enters the sense-dusts without confusion. Overcoming every obstruction, it shines through every empty dharma. Leaving discriminating conditioning, enter clean, clear wisdom and romp and play in *samādhi*. What could be wrong? This is how one must genuinely investigate the essence.

Stepping from the Cliff's Edge

Practice in emptiness and forget conditioning as dazzling light gleams from the shadows. When each portion of spirit is luminous and unhindered, the mind of the three times is interrupted and the four material elements are in balance. Transparent and marvelously bright, in solitary glory for multitudinous *kalpas*, a patch-robed monk can practice like this and not be bound by life and death. In upright practice let go from the edge of the high cliff, not grabbing anything. The ropes around your feet are severed. In wholeness take one step. The buddhas and ancestors all do not reach one's own genuine, wondrously illuminating field, which is called one's self. At this juncture sustain the family business. Just when involved in deliberations, turn around from the stream of thoughts. Empty with enduring spirit, pure with enduring illumination, clear and white, reed flowers and bright moonlight are mixed together. Oars pulled in, the solitary boat drifts past without difficulty. At this time please tell me, who would be anxious to display the eye of discrimination?

Turning the Wheel and the Flavor of Serenity

Traveling around in completion without center or edges, cutting away corners, the circle revolves leaving no residue in the empty cave. In the clear sky of autumn the moon is cold, its radiance bathing the night. The perfect weather of spring is embroidered clouds and elegant flowers. The gateway is open and can be passed through. The wheel of energetic attention turns back to the particulars. All this is the affair that patch-robed monks accept as their own function. No sense-dusts can screen you. The ten thousand dharmas are the mind's light. Step by step go beyond [fixed] location. Unimpeded on the bird's path, just respond to each event of the world.[47] The valley spirit does not toil, but essentially it cannot be confused. Its purpose cannot be matched. Moment to moment from the beginning, all dusts, all minds, and all thoughts are without extraneous forms. The one simple true brightness is persistent. The inner function acquires the marvelous opportunity to display the gathering and rolling up of your residual conditioning. The single bright self is sharpened and cleansed until it is without flaw. Sweep away and disperse classifications. If you understand on your own and just shine, the flavor of serenity can spread. Wisdom arrives inside the circle; affairs are left outside the gate. This is the single profundity beyond birth and death. You must take the backward step and return home. Sincerely I relate these words.

The Family Business

Patch-robed monks roam the world constantly emptying and expanding their minds. Without the slightest remnant held inside, they can respond appropriately, not hindered by beings, not tangled up by dharmas. Openly appearing and disappearing you can freely share, but if merely involved in intellect you will be buried. If embodying pure maturity, then you can naturally journey at ease among the ten thousand changes without touching them and without turning away from them.[48] Box and cover [join] and arrowpoints [meet], harmoniously hitting the mark. Whether releasing or gathering up externals, eliminate all leaking. Such a person can fulfill the family business. From this place just return. The white clouds enter the valley and the bright moon circles the mountain. On this occasion you have the same substance as the elders. So it is said that three people are propped up by one staff and lie down in one bed. Do not leave any traces, and inside and outside will merge into one totality, as leisurely as the sky clearing of rainclouds, as deep as the water drenching the autumn. All of you virtuous people, remember this matter well.

The Amazing Living Beings

Our house is a single field, clean, vast, and lustrous, clearly self-illuminated. When the spirit is vacant without conditions, when awareness is serene without cogitation, then buddhas and ancestors appear and disappear transforming the world. Amid living beings is the original place of nirvana.[49] How amazing it is that all people have this but cannot polish it into bright clarity.[50] In darkness unawakened, they make foolishness cover their wisdom and overflow. One remembrance of illumination can break through and leap out of the dust of *kalpas*. Radiant and clear white, [the single field] cannot be diverted or altered in the three times; the four elements cannot modify it. Solitary glory is deeply preserved, enduring throughout ancient and present times, as the merging of sameness and difference becomes the entire creation's mother. This realm manifests the energy of the many thousands of beings, all appearances merely this [field's] shadows. Truly embody this reality.

Perfect Wandering

The eye that engages the fluctuations and the body that voyages over the world are empty and spirited, still and illuminating, and appear extraordinary among the ten thousand forms. They cannot be buried in the earth's dust and cannot be bundled in the cocoon of past conditioning.[51] The moon traverses the sky, the clouds depart the valley, reflecting without mind, operating without self, becoming radiant and benevolent. This is how everything is perfect, cast off fully and functioning freely. This is called the body emerging from inside the gate.[52] Still this must be embodied while you continue the family business. Emptiness is your seat, stillness is your shelter. Subtly maintained without being existent, it does not involve conditioning; genuinely illuminating without being nonexistent, it does not fall into quantification. Alone and splendid within the circle, profoundly revolving beyond all measure, perfect wandering is guided by the spirits. The great square is without corners.[53] Here you exert energy and, naturally without impediments, comprehend all the shiftings and accept your function.

The Solitary Beacon and the Single Road

People of the Way journey through the world responding to conditions, carefree and without restraint. Like clouds finally raining, like moonlight following the current, like orchids growing in shade, like spring arising in everything, they act without mind, they respond with certainty. This is how perfected people behave. Then they must resume their travels and follow the ancestors, walking ahead with steadiness and letting go of themselves with innocence. The solitary beacon is without companions. The piercing, awe-inspiring voice on the single road to the other shore instantly can fulfill center or borders and pervade from top to bottom. Killing or giving life, rolling up or unrolling, is your own independent decision.

Positive and Appropriate Activity

Expansive and inherently spiritual, refined and inherently bright, [awakened mind] can permeate universally without grasping the merit of its illumination, and can apprehend with-

33

out being bound by discursive thinking. Emerging from manifestations of existence and nonexistence, surpassing the emotions of deliberation and discussion, merely interact positively and appropriately without dependence on others. All buddhas, all ancestors, all leaves, and all flowers relate in this manner. When responding they do not grasp at forms, where illuminating they do not attach to conditions. Then they can stay wide open and unhampered. Only this family wind [intimate awareness] appears complete everywhere. Let yourself accept it.

A Complaint about Bodhidharma's Coming from the West

Attaining the skin and attaining the marrow are only recently established as stages.[54] Arranging the leaves and arranging the flowers become a flowing display. Patch-robed monks who understand complain about the Founder's coming from the west and creating much ado.[55] From this juncture branches have grown, leaving flakes in everyone's eyes. Then various people cut open their heads to create boundless cleverness and engraved their boats to mark where their swords fell overboard. By following them, how can you ever act appropriately? Just right now directly release, drop off, and totally let go. Not a single hair or grain of rice can impede your finally renewing and straightening yourself. Readily you can now cast away everything. The circle integrates brightness; its spirit triumphs in wonder. Simply know that originally it is without defect and not even a bit is excluded. Language cannot reach it, hearing and seeing cannot touch it. It is like a one-horned bison charging through, like a pregnant oyster. In this single beam of light you genuinely wander in practice. Use your vitality to embody this.

The Sixth Ancestor Thoroughly Illuminating

When the Buddha Ancestors first appeared there were no monks and laypeople, but everybody had their own truth and position. When they intimately experienced and genuinely attained, it was called entering the Buddha Mind School.[56] Old Lu [the Sixth Ancestor Huineng], who penetrated the dharma's source, was a person who sold firewood. As soon as he arrived at Huangmei [the Fifth Ancestor's place], he said, "I want to be a buddha."[57] In the rice hulling room the Ancestor [Huineng] worked pounding rice until his mind mirror transcended worldly impurity and he was thoroughly self-illuminated.[58] He was bequeathed the ancestral robe at midnight, and crossed the Dayu Mountains. With faith in the robe, he set it down. Venerable [Hui] Ming with his mighty strength could not lift it and then knew that each person must intimately experience and authentically realize for himself.[59] So nowadays please do not acquiesce to sages and exalt their worth [instead of realizing it yourself]. This is how you should wear the robe and eat your food. When constantly mindful with no distracting considerations, minds do not allow contaminating attachments. Cast off the body of the empty *kalpa*; let go from the steep cliff. Comprehend your sense-object faculties until they are exhausted from top to bottom. Solitary brightness is the only illumination; extensive penetration preserves the marvel. Naturally the mind flowers and radiance shines forth, responding to the visible lands and fields. How could you have ever separated from the various permutations? Now you can enter among diverse beings and travel the bird's way without hindrance, free at last.

The Liberating Eye's Authentic View

Monks of our house must have a dried body and cool mind in order to leap over and cast away birth and death. Discern the mirror's utter depths, vacant and intense, perfectly illuminated. Break out from the four elements and five *skāndhas*.[60] When causes and conditions are not yet in effect, the sense gates not yet matured, the embryo not yet fully developed, and emotions and consciousness not yet flowing, if you still exercise your eye even then, how can suffering not be finished? Realize this fully. The ancestral masters' nostrils and patch-robed monks' life pulse consists of holding firmly and then releasing in activity so that we all discover our own freedom. So it is said that false [thinking] is stopped and stillness necessarily arises, stillness arises and wisdom appears, wisdom arises and stillness necessarily disappears [in wisdom's active functioning]. Clear and distinct, this is the only authentic view.

Graciously Share Yourself

In the great rest and great halting the lips become moldy and mountains of grass grow on your tongue. Moving straight ahead [beyond this state], totally let go, washed clean and ground to a fine polish. Respond with brilliant light to such unfathomable depths as the waters of autumn or the moon stamped in the sky. Then you must know there is a path on which to turn yourself around. When you do turn yourself around you have no different face that can be recognized. Even if you do not recognize [your face], still nothing can hide it. This is penetrating from the topmost all the way down to the bottom. When you have thoroughly investigated your roots back to their ultimate source, a thousand or ten thousand sages are no more than footprints on the trail. In wonder return to the journey, avail yourself of the path and walk ahead. In light there is darkness; where it operates no traces remain. With the hundred grass tips in the busy marketplace graciously share yourself. Wide open and accessible, walking along, casually mount the sounds and straddle the colors while you transcend listening and surpass watching. Perfectly unifying in this manner is simply a patch-robed monk's appropriate activity.

The Genuine Field

The primal mind transcends conditioning, the primal dharma does not speak, but all buddhas and all ancestors are not detained here. In the second gate of meaning [that of the relative and of speech], they engage in dialogue and energy is aroused, which is instantly extracted and dispensed both to the first-class practitioner and to the dull person.[61] Therefore Deshan says that our school has no language and also has not a single dharma for anyone.[62] Originally the people arrived at the truth themselves and affirmed it themselves. Then they began to discuss it only in order to straighten up and clean out forthrightly obsessive thinking and distraction. If such contamination is purified, then vast radiance without barriers has no middle or edge. Circling and spreading out, the light is glistening white, its illumination pervading the ten directions. Sit in meditation and entirely cut off causes and conditioning and language of the three times. Reaching this you cannot attach to a single dust mote. Only in silent serenity is the self known, full-spirited in its own glory, no stranger to sages, not diminished with worldly people. From the beginning only this is the single affair of the old home. How can you possibly attain anything outside yourself? This is called the genuine field where awakened people immediately can respond to the ten thousand changes and enter every realm. Wondrous function and spiritual penetration naturally are without any obstruction at all.

Casting Off All Duality

Purity without stain is your body; perfect illumination without conditioning is your eyes. The eye inside the body does not involve sense gates; the body inside the eye does not collect appearances. So it is said that there is no wisdom outside suchness that can awaken suchness. Moreover, there is no suchness outside wisdom that can be awakened by wisdom. This may be called, buddha is the dharma family's buddha, dharma is the buddha family's dharma. Patch-robed monks arrive here and then know that to follow buddha's utterances and to follow dharma's blossoming is to attain buddhadharma. Restoring the absolute, they all sit and cut off any duality. Only this is what people from ancient to present times have needed to celebrate fully.

RELIGIOUS VERSES

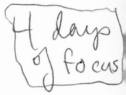

The Acupuncture Needle of Za̧zen [1]

The essential function of all buddhas,
the functional essence of all ancestors,
is to know without touching things
and to illuminate without encountering objects.
Knowing without touching things,
this knowledge is innately subtle.
Illuminating without encountering objects,
this illumination is innately miraculous.
The knowledge innately subtle
has never engaged in discriminating thinking.
The illumination innately miraculous
has never displayed the slightest identification.
Never engaging in discriminating thinking,
this knowledge is rare without match.
Never displaying the most minute identification,

this illumination is complete without grasping.
The water is clear right down to the bottom,
fish lazily swim on.
The sky is vast without end,
birds fly far into the distance.

nature

The Five Ranks

The Partial within the True:
The blue sky clears and the River of Stars' cold flood dries up.
At midnight the wooden boy pounds on the moon's door.
In darkness the jade woman is startled from her sleep.[2]

The True within the Partial:
Ocean and clouds rendezvous at the top of the spirit mountain.
The old woman returns with hair hanging down like white silk
And shyly faces the mirror coldly reflecting her image.

Coming from within the True:
In the moonlit night the huge sea monster sheds its scales.
Its great back rubs the heaven, and it scatters clouds with its
    wing feathers.
Soaring here and there along the bird's path[3]—it is difficult to
    classify.

Coming from within Both Together:
Meeting face to face we need not shun each other's names.
In the changing wind, no injury to the profound meaning.
In the light, a road to the natural differences.

Arriving within Both Together:
The Big Dipper slants across the sky before dawn.
In dewy cold the crane begins to wake from its dreams.
As it flies out of the old nest, the pine tree up in the clouds falls
    over.

The Four Guests and Hosts [4]

The Guest within the Guest:
The affair at the heart of a whole life knits up the eyebrows.
The dust has blown over the whole face and the temples have
     grayed.
As always, going out of the gate without artifice,
How can one continue on today's destitute road?

The Host within the Guest:
No longer yearning for commercial profits or abundant gold;
Evening comes to the ancient road and I ask for news of home.
Having heard reports of the parents' health,
I try to manage difficulties and balance the mind's joy and dread.

The Guest within the Host:
Up in the tower a horn blows to the six bright streets.
On a golden horse the general leaves the Imperial Palace.
Beyond the frontiers his transformative power is sharply
     beneficial.
Not harming anyone, he brings a peaceful age.

The Host within the Host:
Without disturbing the golden sun, ten thousand virtues are
     perfected.
The palace moss, without design, contains the moon.
Above all, avoid speaking the forbidden name of the Emperor.
Who would presume even once to offend the sage's countenance?

The Truth Body[5]

When a flower falls it is autumn.
Where there is no romance is the most romantic.
The wooden man takes the backward step and the golden cord
    is severed.
Clearly there is no opportunity to pull along the iron ox.

The Response Body[6]

With the dice on the tray I trust my luck will prevail.
The wind blows and the grass bends, the crescent moon is in the
   clear sky.
Blocking the street, obstructing the alley, is this ludicrous skin
   bag.
When could Maitreya ever not appear?[7]

The Body Emerging from within the Gate

The true man of no rank is a slab of red meat.[8]
Great thousands of realms of sand are manifest on the tip of a
    hair.
Obviously it is a matter of not borrowing from someone else's
    house.
This is how all achievement functions.

The Gate Emerging from within the Body

Let go of emptiness and come back to the brambly forest.
Riding backward on the ox, drunken and singing,
Who could dislike the misty rain pattering on your bamboo
    raincoat and hat?
In the empty space you cannot stick a needle.

Memorial in Homage to the Third Ancestor, Zen Master Zhijian[9]

The Way is without picking or choosing;[10]
    The waters are deep and the mountains steep.
The Ancestor does not appear or disappear.
    The moon is cold in the blue sky.
The unsprouting branches are awakened with spring flowers.
The tree top without shadows is the spiritual bird's dwelling.
The heavenly pillar so high and lofty;
    The River of Stars flows pure.
The stone ox roars!
    From the cave the clouds arise freely.[11]

Memorial in Homage to the Fourth Ancestor, Zen Master Dayi

The ancestral way was already transmitted
    to Huangmei in his youth.[12]
Empty bubbles suddenly pop,
    pure and clean with no shape.
The true form is magnificently illuminated with gleaming fire.
The teaching's voice is total silence amid the ringing wind
    chimes.
The moon hangs in the old pine tree, cold in the falling night.
The chilled crane in its nest in the clouds has not yet been
    aroused from its dreams.

Memorial in Homage to the Fifth Ancestor, Zen Master Daman

Huangmei's fruit ripened
   and the white lotus flower blossomed.
With inquiry and response the buddha nature
   is planted in different human births.[13]
The robe transmitted to the southern mountain range, he could
     go away.
To the old pine tree on the western mountain range I can come
     again.[14]
Twice borrowing a skin bag to complete this affair;
One jug holds the wind and moon, deep without dust.

Memorial in Homage to Zen Master Touzi Qing

Buried in the stupa are jade bones.[15]
    The clouds embrace the middle of the mountain.
Traces of dust from outside are ended.
    The light of the Way illuminates the core.
Piercing the eye of the golden needle with jade thread,
He continues to create the harmony of the phoenix.
The vessel of spring appears
    and the flowers are fragrant on the withered tree.
At night the crane calls
    and moonlight drenches the solitary nest.
The style of the house so tasteless and thin,
    the stone ox swallows the waters.
The descendants so flourishing,
    the heavenly pillar touches the zenith.

In Praise of Master Furong, True Ancestor

With phoenix eyes and crane body,
    a powerful worker in the ancestral gate,
He awakened beings beyond measure;
    even before speaking there was drumming and singing.[16]
Receiving his orders, with his long sword he trusted to heaven.
Responding to changes, the bright pearl was in the palm of his
    hand.
The supreme emptiness has the moonlight.
    The old rabbit tastes the frost.[17]
The great ocean is without wind.
    The glorious whale blows a spout.

Guidepost of Silent Illumination

Silent and serene, forgetting words, bright clarity appears
    before you.
When you reflect it you become vast, where you embody it you
    are spiritually uplifted.
Spiritually solitary and shining, inner illumination restores
    wonder,
Dew in the moonlight, a river of stars, snow-covered pines,
    clouds enveloping the peak.
In darkness it is most bright, while hidden it is all the more
    manifest.
The crane dreams in the wintery mists. The autumn waters flow
    far into the distance.
Endless *kalpas* are totally empty, all things completely the same.
When the wonder exists in serenity, all achievement is forgotten
    in illumination.
What is this wonder? Alertly seeing through confusion
Is the way of silent illumination and the origin of subtle
    radiance.
Vision penetrating into subtle radiance is weaving gold on a
    jade loom.[18]
The upright and the inclined yield to each other; light and dark
    are interdependent.[19]
Not depending on sense faculty and object, at the right time
    they interact.
Drink the medicine of good views. Beat the poison-smeared
    drum.
When they interact, killing and giving life are up to you.
Through the gate the self emerges and the branches bear fruit.

Only silence is the supreme speech, only illumination is the
    universal response.
Responding without falling into achievement, speaking
    without involving listeners,
The ten thousand forms majestically glisten and expound the
    dharma.
All objects certify it, every one in dialogue.
Dialoguing and certifying, they respond appropriately to each
    other;
But if illumination neglects serenity, then aggressiveness
    appears.
Certifying and dialoguing, they respond to each other
    appropriately;
But if serenity neglects illumination, murkiness leads to wasted
    dharma.
When silent illumination is fulfilled, the lotus blossoms, the
    dreamer awakens,
A hundred streams flow into the ocean, a thousand ranges face
    the highest peak.
Like geese preferring milk, like bees gathering nectar,
When silent illumination reaches the ultimate, I offer my
    teaching.
The teaching of silent illumination penetrates from the highest
    down to the foundation.
The body being *sunyata*, the arms in *mudrā*;[20]
From beginning to end the changing appearances and ten
    thousand differences have one pattern.
Mr. Ho offered jade [to the Emperor; Minister] Xiangru pointed
    to its flaws.[21]
Facing changes has its principles, the great function is without
    striving.

The ruler stays in the kingdom, the general goes beyond the
   frontiers.
Our school's affair hits the mark straight and true.
Transmit it to all directions without desiring to gain credit.

Guidepost for the Hall of Pure Bliss

By seeking appearances and sounds one cannot truly find the
    Way.
The deep source of realization
    comes with constancy, bliss, self, and purity.
Its purity is constant, its bliss is myself.
The two are mutually dependent, like firewood and fire.
The self's bliss is not exhausted, constant purity has no end.
Deep existence is beyond forms.
    Wisdom illuminates the inside of the circle.
Inside the circle the self vanishes,
    neither existent nor nonexistent.
Intimately conveying spiritual energy,
    it subtly turns the mysterious pivot.
When the mysterious pivot finds the opportunity to turn,
    the original light auspiciously appears.
When the mind's conditioning has not yet sprouted,
    how can words and images be distinguished?
Who is it that can distinguish them?
    Clearly understand and know by yourself.
Whole and inclusive with inherent insight,
    it is not concerned with discriminating thought.
When discriminating thought is not involved,
    it is like white reed flowers shining in the snow.
One beam of light's gleam permeates the vastness.
The gleam permeates through all directions,
    from the beginning not covered or concealed.
Catching the opportunity to emerge,
    amid transformations it flourishes.

Following appropriately amid transformations,
    the pure bliss is unchanged.
The sky encompasses it, the ocean seals it,
    every moment without deficiency.
In the achievement without deficiency
    inside and outside are interfused.
All dharmas transcend their limits, all gates are wide open.
Through the open gates are the byways of playful wandering.
Dropping off senses and sense objects is like
    the flowers of our gazing and listening falling away.
Gazing and listening are only distant conditions
    of thousands of hands and eyes.
The others die from being too busy, but I maintain continuity.
In the wonder of continuity
    are no traces of subtle identifications.
Within purity is bliss, within silence is illumination.
The house of silent illumination is the hall of pure bliss.
Dwelling in peace and forgetting hardship,
    let go of adornments and become genuine.
The motto for becoming genuine:
    nothing is gained by speaking.
The goodness of Vimalakirti enters the gate of nonduality.[22]

APPENDIX A

Song of the Grass-Roof Hermitage by Shitou

This poem by Shitou Xiqian (700–790) presents an important early model for Sōtō Zen practice which influenced Hongzhi's silent illumination. (From Taishō Shinshū Daizōkyō *[Toyko: Taishō Issaikyō Kankōkai, 1924–33], 51:461c. This first published English translation, by Taigen Daniel Leighton and Kazuaki Tanahashi, appeared originally in* Windbell *[1985].)*

I've built a grass hut where there's nothing of value.
After eating, I relax and enjoy a nap.
When it was completed, fresh weeds appeared.
Now it's been lived in—covered by weeds.
The person in the hut lives here calmly,
not stuck to inside, outside, or in between.
Places worldly people live, he doesn't live.
Realms worldly people love, he doesn't love.
Though the hut is small, it includes the entire world.
In ten square feet, an old man illumines forms and their
    nature.
A Great Vehicle bodhisattva trusts without doubt.
The middling or lowly can't help wondering;
Will this hut perish or not?

Perishable or not, the original master is present,
not dwelling south or north, east or west.
Firmly based on steadiness, it can't be surpassed.
A shining window below the green pines—
jade palaces or vermilion towers can't compare with it.
Just sitting with head covered all things are at rest.
Thus, this mountain monk doesn't understand at all.
Living here he no longer works to get free.
Who would proudly arrange seats, trying to entice
        guests?
Turn around the light to shine within, then just return.
The vast inconceivable source can't be faced or turned
        away from.
Meet the ancestral teachers, be familiar with their
        instruction,
bind grasses to build a hut, and don't give up.
Let go of hundreds of years and relax completely.
Open your hands and walk, innocent.
Thousands of words, myriad interpretations,
are only to free you from obstructions.
If you want to know the undying person in the hut,
don't separate from this skin bag here and now.

APPENDIX B

Sōtō Lineage: Bodhidharma to Dōgen[1]

Bodhidharma (5th–6th cent.)
Awakening Teaching   Bodaidaruma
|

Dazu Huike (487–593)
Great Ancestor *Prajñā* (Insight) Ability   Taisō Eka
|

Jianzhi Sengcan (d. 606)
Mirror Wisdom Gem of the Community   Kanchi Sōsan
|

Dayi Daoxin (580–651)
Great Medicine Faith Way   Dai-i Dōshin
|

Daman Hongren (602–675)
Great Fullness Broad Endurance   Daiman Kōnin
↓

1. Based on Dōgen's lineage as accepted in the Japanese Sōtō school. Chinese monks' names are given (except Sanskrit for Bodhidharma and Japanese for Dōgen) followed by dates (where known), English translation, and Japanese pronunciation. See Introduction, note 1.

Dajian Huineng (638–713)
Great Mirror *Prajñā* Talent   Daikan Enō

Qingyuan Xingsi (d. 740)
Green Source Walking Contemplation   Seigen Gyōshi

Shitou Xiqian (700–790)
Above the Rock Rare Transformation   Sekitō Kisen

Yaoshan Weiyen (745–828)
Medicine Mountain Majestic Consideration   Yakusan Igen

Yunyan Tansheng (781–841)
Cloud Cliff Dim Splendor   Ungan Donjō

Dongshan Liangjie (807–869)
Cave Mountain Virtuous Servant   Tōzan Ryōkai

Yunju Daoying (d. 902)   Caoshan Benji (840–901)
Cloud Dwelling Way Sustainer   Cao Mountain Primal Silence
Ungō Dōyō   Sōzan Honjaku

Tongan Daopi (n.d.)
Uniform Peace Great Way   Dōan Dōhi

Tongan Guanzhi (n.d.)
Uniform Peace Determined Contemplation   Dōan Kanshi

Liangshan Yuanguan (n.d.)
Bridge Mountain Contemplating Conditions   Ryōzan Enkan
↓

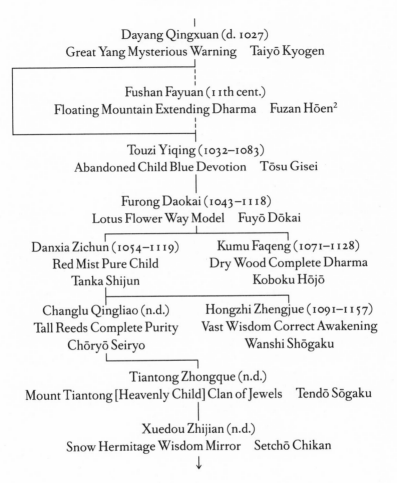

Dayang Qingxuan (d. 1027)
Great Yang Mysterious Warning   Taiyō Kyogen

Fushan Fayuan (11th cent.)
Floating Mountain Extending Dharma   Fuzan Hōen[2]

Touzi Yiqing (1032–1083)
Abandoned Child Blue Devotion   Tōsu Gisei

Furong Daokai (1043–1118)
Lotus Flower Way Model   Fuyō Dōkai

Danxia Zichun (1054–1119)
Red Mist Pure Child
Tanka Shijun

Kumu Faqeng (1071–1128)
Dry Wood Complete Dharma
Koboku Hōjō

Changlu Qingliao (n.d.)
Tall Reeds Complete Purity
Chōryō Seiryo

Hongzhi Zhengjue (1091–1157)
Vast Wisdom Correct Awakening
Wanshi Shōgaku

Tiantong Zhongque (n.d.)
Mount Tiantong [Heavenly Child] Clan of Jewels   Tendō Sōgaku

Xuedou Zhijian (n.d.)
Snow Hermitage Wisdom Mirror   Setchō Chikan

2. Fushan, a Rinzai master, transmitted and thereby preserved the Sōtō teaching without accepting the transmission himself. When Dayang outlived his enlightened disciples, the lineage was about to die out; but the aged Dayang enlisted the aid of Fushan, already a successor to the Rinzai line six generations after Rinzai. Fushan was in complete dharmic accord with Dayang, but felt that he could not take on the additional responsibilities of publicly proclaiming the Sōtō style. However, Fushan was able to transmit the Sōtō teaching to an able student, Touzi Yiqing.

|

Tiantong Rujing (1163–1228)
Mount Tiantong Pure Suchness   Tendō Nyōjō

|

Eihei Dōgen (1200–1253)
Eternal Peace Way Source

APPENDIX C

Wade-Giles Transliterations for Chinese Names

Pinyin	*Wade-Giles Transliteration*
Caodong	Ts'ao tung
Caoshan Benji	Ts'ao shan Pen chi
Changlu Qingliao	Ch'ang lu Ch'ing liao
Congdao	Tsung tao
Dahui Zonggao	Ta hui Tsung kao
Dajian Huineng	Ta chien Hui neng
Daman Hongren	Ta man Hung jen
Danxia Zichun	Tan hsia Tzu ch'un
Dayang Qingxuan	Ta ying Ch'ing hsuan
Dayi Daoxin	Ta i Tao hsin
Dazu Huike	Ta su Hui ko
Deshan Xuanjian	Te shan Hsuan chien
Desun	Te sun
Dongling Yungyu	Tung ling Yung yu
Dongming Huiji	Tung ming Hui chih
Dongshan Liangjie	Tung shan Liang chieh
Furong Daokai	Fu jung Tao k'ai
Fushan Fayuan	Fou shan Fa yuan
Guishan Lingyou	Kuei shan Ling yu

Hongzhi Zhengjue	Hung chih Cheng chueh
Huanglong Huinan	Huang lung Hui nan
Jianzhi Sengcan	Chien chih Seng tsan
Jinhua Juzhi	Chin hua Chu chi
Kumu Faqeng	K'u mu Fa ch'eng
Laozi	Lao tzu
Liangshan Yuanguan	Liang shan Yuan guan
Linji Yixuan	Lin chi I hsuan
Mazu Dao-i	Ma tsu Tao i
Nanquan Puyuan	Nan chuan P'u yuan
Puqung	P'u ch'ung
Qingyuan Xingsi	Ch'ing yuan Hsing ssu
Sengzhao	Seng chao
Shangshan	Hsiang shan
Shitou Xiqian	Shih t'ou Hsi ch'ien
Si-de Huihui	Tzu te Hui hui
Tiantong Rujing	T'ien t'ung Ju ching
Tiantong Zhongque	T'ien t'ung Chung ch'ueh
Tongan Daopi	T'ung an Tao p'i
Tongan Guanzhi	T'ung an Kuan chi
Touzi Yiqing	T'ou tzu I ch'ing
Wansong Xingxiu	Wan sung Hsing hsiu
Xuansha Shibei	Hsuan sha Shi pei
Xuedou Zhijian	Hsueh tou Chih chien
Yaoshan Weiyen	Yao shan Wei yen
Yuanwu Keqin	Yuan wu K'o ch'in
Yunju Daoying	Yun chu Tao ying
Yunyan Tansheng	Yun yen T'an sheng
Zaisong Daozhe	Tsai sung Tao che
Zhaozhou Congshen	Chao chou Ts'ung shen

NOTES

Introduction

1. Principal sources for Hongzhi's life are *Xu Chuan Deng Lu* [Later Record of the Transmission of the Lamp], in *Taishō Shinshū Daizōkyō* (Tokyo: Taishō Issaikyō Kankōkai, 1924–1933), no. 2077, vol. 51, p. 579; Isshū Miura and Ruth Fuller Sasaki, *Zen Dust: The History of the Koan and Koan Study in Rinzai (Lin-chi) Zen* (New York: Harcourt, Brace & World, 1966), pp. 170–171; Takashi James Kodera, *Dōgen's Formative Years in China: An Historical Study and Annotated Translation of the "Hōkyō-ki."* (Boulder, Colo.: Prajñā Press, 1980), pp. 92–93, 99–101; and Dan Stevenson, "Silent Illumination Ch'an," *Ch'an Magazine* (Elmhurst, N.Y.) 2, no. 5 (1981).

Throughout the Introduction, when persons are first mentioned, their dates (when available) are provided in the text. English translations of names and Japanese pronunciations of Chinese names commonly used in Japanese Zen are provided in the Sōtō Lineage (Appendix B) or, for prominent persons not in that lineage, in the notes. Monks' names, usually given to Zen monks by their ordination masters, often reflect aspects of their spiritual character and potentiality (not unlike Native American names). However, it was also common to later use a name derived from a place where a master taught; these do not generally refer to individuals' spiritual qualities. The translations provided here may not reflect every relevant spiritual meaning or connotation of the names.

2. Linji and Caodong are the two main surviving branches of Chinese Chan Buddhism, in Japanese Zen called Rinzai and Sōtō.

3. The Flower Ornament Sutra is called the Avatamsaka in Sanskrit, Huayen in Chinese, and Kegon in Japanese. A distinct Huayen school developed in China based on this sutra. These teachings are discussed in the "Sōtō Context" section of the Introduction, below.

4. The self before the empty *kalpa*, when the material universe does not yet exist, is considered one's essential nature. It is a common Zen expression for probing true self or ultimate understanding, synonymous for the original face, or your face before your parents were born. *Kalpa* is Sanskrit for a vast duration of time (see note 12 to the Practice Instructions). In Buddhist cosmology each universe exists for a cycle of four *kalpas*: the empty, the becoming, the abiding, and the decaying.

5. Yuanwu's name means "Complete Enlightenment Able and Diligent," in Japanese pronounced Engo Kassan. For an English translation of his famous collection, see Thomas Cleary and J. C. Cleary, trans., *The Blue Cliff Record*, 3 vols. (Boulder, Colo.: Shambhala, 1977). Hereafter I will use the term "koan" to refer to these stories, a word now familiar in English usage.

6. Shohaku Okumura, trans., *"Shōbōgenzō Zuimonki": Sayings of Eihei Dōgen Zenji, Recorded by Koun Ejō* (Kyoto: Kyoto Sōtō Zen Center, 1987), sec. 2–6, p. 77.

7. Dahui Zonggao means "Great Wisdom Ancestral Shining Sun"; in Japanese, Daie Sōkō.

8. Miura and Sasaki, *Zen Dust*, p. 171.

9. Dachuan Puji, ed., *Wu Deng Hui Yuan* (Taipei: Guang Wen Bookstore, 1971).

10. Principal sources for this section are Chang Chung-Yuan, trans., *Original Teachings of Ch'an Buddhism: Selected from "Transmission from the Lamp"* (New York: Vintage Books, 1971), including his introductions; Thomas Cleary, ed. and trans., *Timeless Spring: A Sōtō Zen*

Anthology (Tokyo: Weatherhill, 1980); Thomas Cleary, trans., *Transmission of Light: Zen in the Art of Enlightenment by Zen Master Keizan* (San Francisco: North Point Press, 1990); Thomas Cleary, trans., *The Book of Serenity* (Hudson, N.Y.: Lindisfarne Press, 1990); William F. Powell, trans., *The Record of Tung-shan* (Honolulu: University of Hawaii Press, 1986); Kazuaki Tanahashi, ed., *Moon in a Dewdrop: Writings of Zen Master Dōgen* (San Francisco: North Point Press, 1985); and Alfonso Verdu, *Dialectical Aspects in Buddhist Thought: Studies in Sino-Japanese Mahāyāna Idealism* (Lawrence: University of Kansas, Center for East Asian Studies, 1974).

Mazu Dao-i means "Horse Ancestor Way of Oneness"; in Japanese, Baso Dōitsu.

11. Sengzhao, a disciple of the great translator Kumārajīva (344–413), was a master of Mādhyamika, the early Mahāyāna Buddhist teaching focusing on minute analysis of emptiness.

12. T. Cleary, *Book of Serenity*, case 91, p. 391.

13. See T. Cleary, *Timeless Spring*, pp. 36–38. "The Merging of Difference and Unity" is called "Can Tong Qi" in Chinese, "Sandōkai" in Japanese.

14. For the "Song of the Jewel Mirror Samādhi" ("Bao Jing Sanmei" in Chinese, "Hōkyō Zammai" in Japanese), see T. Cleary, *Timeless Spring*, pp. 39–42. For Dongshan's verse commentaries on the five ranks, see Powell, *Record of Tung-shan*, pp. 61–63.

15. For further discussions of the five ranks, see Verdu, *Dialectical Aspects in Buddhist Thought*; T. Cleary, *Timeless Spring*, pp. 36–53; Chang, *Original Teachings of Ch'an*, pp. 41–57; and Powell, *Record of Tung-shan*, pp. 11–14. For Rinzai school treatment of the five ranks, see Miura, *The Zen Koan* (abridged republication of *Zen Dust*), pp. 62–72.

16. From T. Cleary, *Timeless Spring*, p. 36.

17. Nanquan Puyuan means "South Fountain Universal Vow"; in Japanese, Nansen Fugan. See note 8 to the Practice Instructions below. Guishan Lingyou means "Practice Mountain Spiritual Protection"; in Japanese, Isan Reiyū. Guishan is considered one of the founders

of the Guiyang school of Zen, one of the classical "five houses," which include Sōtō and Rinzai.

18. Later a monk asked Dongshan whether Yunyan himself knew it is or not. Dongshan answered, "If he didn't know it is, how could he be able to say this? If he did know it is, how could he be willing to say this?" (T. Cleary, *Book of Serenity*, case 49, p. 206).

19. Principal sources for this section are J. C. Cleary, trans., *Swampland Flowers: The Letters and Lectures of Zen Master Ta Hui* (New York: Grove Press, 1977); Takashi James Kodera, "Ta Hui Tsung-Kao (1089–1163) and His 'Introspecting the Kung-An Ch'an (Koan Zen),'" *Ohio Journal of Religious Studies* (Cleveland) 6, no. 1 (1978); Kodera, *Dogen's Formative Years in China*; and Miura and Sasaki, *Zen Dust*.

Linji Yixuan is a fourth-generation descendant of Mazu. His name means "Near the River Profound Meaning"; in Japanese, Rinzai Gigen.

20. Okumura, *Shōbōgenzō Zuimonki*, p. 193.

21. Cleary and Cleary, *Blue Cliff Record* 1:xxii–xxiii.

22. J. C. Cleary, *Swampland Flowers*, pp. 129, 131.

23. Principal sources for this section include Thomas Cleary, trans., *"Shōbōgenzō": Zen Essays by Dōgen* (Honolulu: University of Hawaii Press, 1986); Tanahashi, *Moon in a Dewdrop*; Shohaku Okumura, trans. and ed., *Dōgen Zen* (Kyoto: Kyoto Sōtō Zen Center, 1988); Yūhō Yokoi, *The Shōbōgenzō* (Tokyo: Sankibō Buddhist Bookstore, 1986); Hee-Jin Kim, *Dōgen Kigen: Mystical Realist* (Tucson: University of Arizona Press, 1975); Shunryu Suzuki, *Zen Mind, Beginner's Mind* (New York: Weatherhill, 1970); Steven Heine, "Dōgen Casts Off 'What': An Analysis of Shinjin Datsuraku," *Journal of the International Association of Buddhist Studies* (Bloomington, Ind.) 9, no. 1 (1986); and Carl Bielefeldt, *Dōgen's Manuals of Zen Meditation* (Berkeley and Los Angeles: University of California Press, 1988).

Si-de Huihui means "Self Realized Radiant Wisdom"; in Japanese, Jitoku Eki. He is known for one of the major traditional series of oxherding verses. Dongming Huiji means "Eastern Brightness

Beneficial Sun"; in Japanese, Tōmyō Enichi. Dongling Yungyu means "Eastern Mound Eternal Giving"; in Japanese, Tōryō Eiyo.

24. See Dōgen's "Zazenshin" (Acupuncture Needle of Zazen), in Bielefeldt, *Dōgen's Manuals*, pp. 199–205; and in Okumura, *Dōgen Zen*, pp. 99–101.

25. Norman Waddell and Masao Abe, "Dōgen's Fukanzazengi and Shō-bōgenzō Zazengi," *Eastern Buddhist* 6, no. 2 (1973): 123.

26. Bielefeldt, *Dōgen's Manuals*, pp. 198–199.

27. His name means "Facing the Mountain Auspicious Direction."

28. Okumura, *Dōgen Zen*, pp. 55–56.

29. Translations of Dōgen's version of this poem include ibid., pp. 100–101; Tanahashi, *Moon in a Dewdrop*, pp. 218–219; and Bielefeldt, *Dōgen's Manuals*, pp. 204–205.

30. Bielefeldt, *Dōgen's Manuals*, p. 205.

31. Waddell and Abe, "Dōgen's Fukanzazengi," p. 122.

32. See ibid., p. 123; Okumura, *Dōgen Zen*, pp. 94–95; and, for a helpful discussion of Dōgen's meditation technique, T. Cleary, *Shōbōgenzō*, pp. 9–13.

33. Bielefeldt, *Dōgen's Manuals*, p. 181.

34. Heine, "Dōgen Casts Off 'What,'" p. 53.

35. T. Cleary, *Shōbōgenzō*, p. 32.

36. Okumura, *Dōgen Zen*, p. 53.

37. Heine, "Dōgen Casts Off 'What,'" pp. 54–55, 61–63.

38. See ibid., pp. 55–56.

39. T. Cleary, *Book of Serenity*, case 67, p. 281.

40. For *genjōkōan* practice, see Kim, *Dōgen Kigen*, p. 100.

41. For examples of Yogācāra teaching, see D. T. Suzuki, trans., *The Laṅkāvatāra Sutra* (Boulder, Colo.: Prajñā Press, 1978); or Yoshito S. Hakeda, trans., *The Awakening of Faith: Attributed to Aśvaghosha* (New York: Columbia University Press, 1967).

42. From T. Cleary, *Timeless Spring*, pp. 36–37.

43. For examples of Deep Ecology, see John Seed, Joanna Macy, Pat Fleming, and Arne Naess, *Thinking Like a Mountain: Towards a Council of All Beings* (Philadelphia: New Society Publishers, 1988); and

Allan Hunt Badiner, ed., *Dharma Gaia: A Harvest of Essays on Buddhism and Ecology* (Berkeley: Parallax Press, 1990).

44. Dongshan, in "The Song of the Jewel Mirror Samādhi"; from T. Cleary, *Timeless Spring*, pp. 39–42.

Practice Instructions

1. A disciple of Hongzhi, whose name means "Universal Respect," Monk Puqung is not mentioned among Hongzhi's eleven most prominent disciples in the *Wu Deng Hui Yuan*. I can find no other reference to him.

2. The mirror is a traditional Zen image for the clear vacant mind reflecting without attachment or discrimination. In his "Song of the Jewel Mirror Samādhi," Dongshan Liangjie, the founder of the Caodong/Sōtō tradition to which Hongzhi is a successor, uses the jeweled mirror as an image of awakened, concentrated mind. See T. Cleary, *Timeless Spring*, pp. 39–42.

3. Taipai Peak was the highest peak on Mount Tiantong, where Hongzhi's Jingde Monastery was located. The three names were used interchangeably for Hongzhi's temple.

4. "Dragons and elephants" is a common Zen image for enlightened practitioners. "Dragon," here and elsewhere in the text, refers to the indigenous Chinese dragon rather than the Indian *nāga*, which Hongzhi mentions later using the standard Chinese transliteration.

5. "Dharma" comes from Sanskrit and refers to the teaching of spiritual realization, to the truth of what is taught, and, as "dharmas," to the particular elements of the field of reality. Here the last meaning is emphasized.

6. The moon is an image for awakening, shining equally on all the streams of phenomena.

7. The phrase "responsive interaction" is used frequently by Hongzhi; it can also mean "appropriate," "union," or "merging." "Box and cover" and "arrowpoints" refer to Shitou's "Merging of Difference and Unity": "Phenomena exist like box and cover joining; principle

accords like arrowpoints meeting." This is an image of the mutual noninterference and unobstructed functioning of phenomena described in Chinese Huayen Buddhist theory. Arrowpoints meeting head on in air depicts the miraculous functioning of the absolute directly in the phenomenal. In the "Song of the Jewel Mirror Samādhi" Dongshan says, "When arrowpoints meet head on, what has this to do with the power of skill." Above quotes are from T. Cleary, *Timeless Spring*, pp. 36–42.

8. This imagery refers to Dongshan's "Song of the Jewel Mirror Samādhi": "For the benefit of those with inferior ability, there is a jeweled footrest and brocade robes; for the benefit of those capable of wonder, a wildcat or white ox" (from Powell, *The Record of Tungshan*, pp. 63–65). Dongshan in this phrase refers back to a saying of one of his early teachers, Nanquan (748–834), a student of Mazu (709–788) and teacher of the great Zhaozhou (778–897). Hongzhi cites it in the *Book of Serenity*, case 69: "Nanquan said to the assembly, 'The Buddhas of past, present, and future do not know it is: cats and cows know it is.'" This case relates to the straightforward, unselfconscious awareness and activity of cats and cows, as compared to those of humans. Both animals are associated with Nanquan, who is famous for the story of his "killing a cat." See Cleary and Cleary, *Blue Cliff Record*, case 63, II:406. Nanquan was fond of referring to oxen, for example stating that after he died he would come back as "a water buffalo down the hill": see Chang, *Original Teachings of Ch'an Buddhism*, pp. 153–163. The ox was later used in Zen in various versions of oxherding pictures that depict stages of spiritual development. In some versions the ox progresses from black to white, representing the purification process. Hongzhi also refers to oxen frequently, sometimes apparently with the oxherding images.

9. "Home-leaver" is a traditional designation for Buddhist monks, referring back to when the historical Buddha, Shākyamuni, left his palace in ancient India to seek and achieve perfected enlightenment. The term also applies to Chinese Zen monks who left their society's rigid family system to enter the monastery or wander from teacher

to teacher. On a deeper spiritual level, home-leaving refers to the practitioner's letting go of attachments derived from personal habitual, psychological, and emotional conditioning.

10. "Patch-robed monk" is a standard epithet for a Buddhist monk, referring to the ordination robe that monks have sewn together since the time of Shākyamuni, originally from discarded rags dyed uniformly.

11. The action of pulling back the ox's nose is pictured in some versions of the oxherding series for the "taming of the ox," a stage of the path often involving arduous purification and training.

12. A *kalpa* is a duration of time described by the image of a bird that flies once every hundred years over the peak of Mount Everest with a piece of silk in her claws: the length of time it would take the silk to wear down the mountain completely is said to be one *kalpa*. For the "empty *kalpa*" in the Buddhist cosmological cycle, see Introduction, note 4.

13. "Bodhi" is a Sanskrit word meaning complete awakening, from the same root as "buddha," the awakened one.

14. The "broad long tongue" is one of the thirty-two physical marks of a buddha, indicating eloquent expression of the truth. "Dharma" is used here to mean the realm of reality and also the teaching that effects its realization.

15. "Two forms" is a conventional name for yin and yang, the ancient Chinese dualism representing earth and heaven, dark and light, passive and active, and female and male, respectively.

16. "Family business" is an image for the perpetuation and transmittal of a particular teaching tradition or lineage. In a broader sense, all those who take refuge in buddhadharma are called "children of buddha," so to carry on the family business means to fulfill one's own innermost heartfelt vow to achieve enlightenment, in the Mahāyāna by liberating all beings together with oneself.

17. "The bottom of the bucket falling out" is a Zen image for the experience of one's preconceptions and fixed world view suddenly and completely evaporating. After such experience one's attitudes are

transformed irrevocably, although ingrained habitual responses may still govern one's conduct to varying extents in the context of further activity in the world.

18. *Samādhi* is the state of meditative concentration. Mahāyāna Buddhist sutras list many different colorfully named *samādhis*.

19. The dharma realm or realm of reality (in Sanskrit, *dharmadhātu*) is the whole field of dharma or truth, equivalent to all dharmas or entities, that is, the entire phenomenal universe seen in its primordial purity.

20. The reference here is to Laozi's *Dao De Qing*, the early Daoist classic, Book 6: "The valley spirit never dies. This is called the mysterious female. The mysterious female's door is called the root of heaven and earth."

21. Ancestors, in some English translations called "patriarchs," refers to the lineage of masters going back to Shākyamuni Buddha, who have maintained and transmitted the teaching. This term especially designates the great founders who established, or developed and spread, branches of the teaching.

22. "A shadow of a hair's gap" is a gap between the self and the arising and extinction of phenomena. Before the gap there is awareness that immediately recognizes the arising of the scenery of sounds, sights, thoughts, and so on.

23. "Grounds, roots, and dusts" refer to the eighteen *dhātus*, that is, the six sense consciousnesses, six sense faculties, and six sense objects, which when combined produce our experience of the phenomenal world.

24. Clouds are an image for home-leaving monks, wandering freely. Dragons are an image for enlightened masters or adepts (see note 4 above).

25. The "backward step" is meditative introspection, the primary technique of Hongzhi's meditation practice, also expounded by Zen teachers such as the Sixth Ancestor Huineng, Shitou, and Dōgen. See the section entitled "Hongzhi's Relation to Dōgen" in the Introduction.

26. In "the self joyfully enters *samādhi* in all delusions and accepts its function," reference is to the *samādhi* of self-enjoyment or fulfillment, an important aspect of Sōtō Zen teachings called *jijuyū zammai* in Japanese; see, for example, "Jijuyū Zammai," in Okumura, *Dōgen Zen*, pp. 43–135. The Chinese compound that means enjoyment or fulfillment translates literally as "receive function." Here Hongzhi repeats the character for function to emphasize the literal meaning.

27. As an idiom, "cauldrons" means simply "uprightness." The cauldron is a traditional Chinese implement for alchemy and cooking and so is associated with spiritual transformation. Here it is an image for the context of meditation practice and its yogic reliability. Cauldron is the name of hexagram 50 in the ancient Chinese classic *Book of Changes*, or *I Qing*: "To change things nothing compares to the cauldron; this is the vessel used to refine the wise, forge sages, cook buddhas, and purify adepts. How could it not be very auspicious and developmental?" (Thomas Cleary, trans., *The Buddhist "I Ching," by Chih-hsu Ou-i* [Boston: Shambhala, 1987], p. 189).

28. The great Zen master Zhaozhou Congshen (778–897; "Zhao Province Obeying Counsel," in Japanese Jōshū Jūshin) is the source of many of the classic koans. When he was approached for instructions by a newly arrived monk, Zhaozhou asked if he had eaten breakfast. When the monk replied affirmatively, Zhaozhou said, "Then go wash your bowl." See Koun Yamada, trans., *Gateless Gate* (Los Angeles: Center Publications), case 7; and Cleary, *Book of Serenity*, case 39, pp. 171–172. Hongzhi's verse commentary to this case in the *Book of Serenity* is:

> Breakfast over, the direction is to wash the bowl;
> Opened up, the mind ground meets of itself.
> And now, a guest of the monastery, having studied to the full—
> But was there enlightenment in there or not?

Hongzhi in this passage of the text also refers to another story about Zhaozhou. Receiving two visiting monks, he asked if they had been there before. When they in turn answered affirmatively and negatively, Zhaozhou responded uniformly to both, "Have a cup of tea." When a monastery official asked about this, Zhaozhou told him also, "Have a cup of tea." See John C. H. Wu, *The Golden Age of Zen* (Taipei: United Publishing Center, 1975), p. 136.

29. The "jade vessel" is an image for pure, enlightened mind. "Turning over on its side" represents the function of awakening, responding to limitations of the phenomenal world ("inclined" is a Sōtō term for the relative contrasted to the absolute). In Buddhism the four elements—earth, water, fire, and air—are traditionally the components of all material.

30. Mountains can be an image for Zen masters, who are often named for the mountains where they reside. "Family wind," or home wind, refers to the flavor or style of teaching of a particular school or lineage.

31. For discussions of the alchemical processes of yin and yang, see Thomas Cleary, trans., *The Taoist I Ching* (Boston: Shambhala, 1986); or Thomas Cleary, trans. and ed., *The Inner Teachings of Taoism* (Boston: Shambhala, 1986).

32. Reference here is to light and shadow as dualistic conceptions.

33. Reference is to Shitou's "Merging of Difference and Unity": "Right in light there is darkness, but don't confront it as darkness; right in darkness there is light, but don't see it as light. Light and dark are relative to one another like forward and backward steps. All things have their function. It is a matter of use in the appropriate situation" (T. Cleary, *Timeless Spring*, p. 37).

34. "River sand" or "pebbles" is conventionally used in Chinese translations of Buddhist sutras to denote "all the grains of sand along the Ganges River," a common phrase in the sutras indicating a vast number. The image here may also include the action of pebbles polishing each other in the current.

35. "Forearm bending back to meet" (literally, "forearm [or elbow] back") is enigmatic but seems to depict a gesture of gathering in or of indicating oneself with forearm drawn back to meet the chest. This appears to be a posture of self-containment, which Hongzhi

recommends as also responsive to events. The "third eye" (literally, "upper gate eye") indicates the spiritual eye of insight usually depicted on the mid-forehead; also the eye of Maheshvara, the king of heavenly deities in Indian cosmology, a name used as an epithet for great bodhisattvas as well.

36. The "white grass tips" is a synonym for the variety of phenomena.

37. This is the utterance of Shitou at the time of his great awakening, "Who can understand myriad things as oneself? Only a sage." See the section entitled "The Sōtō Context" in the Introduction; and Chang, *Original Teachings of Ch'an Buddhism*, p. 245.

38. The "five degrees of achievement" literally reads "meritorious action"; this phrase is used in the Sōtō school for the "five degrees of meritorious achievement," one of two systems of five ranks teachings presented by the school's founder, Dongshan Liangjie (807–869). See the discussion of the five ranks in the Introduction, "The Sōtō Context." Hongzhi's verse commentaries, "The Five Ranks," may be found in the Religious Verses, below.

39. "Mutual union" here could also be translated as "mutual return" or "interaction." The character *ji*, rendered here as "energetic opportunity," is quite versatile: it can denote energy, change, function, opportunity, origin, loom, or mechanism, among its primary meanings. This sentence might also be read, "Here you have the interacting function."

40. Jinhua Juzhi or Judi (9th cent.) means "Golden Flower of Juzhi [a place]"; in Japanese, Kinka Gutei. This Zen master was famous for always responding to questions by raising one finger. See T. Cleary, *Book of Serenity*, case 84; Cleary and Cleary, *Blue Cliff Record*, case 19; and Yamada, *Gateless Gate*, case 3. In the *Book of Serenity*, Hongzhi includes this verse commentary:

> *Old Judi's finger-tip Chan—*
> *Thirty years he used it without wearing it out.*
> *Truly he has the unconventional technique of a man of the Way—*
> *Ultimately there are no mundane things before his eyes to see.*

His realization most simple,
The device the more broad.
An ocean of billions of worlds is drunk in the tip of a hair:
Fish and dragons limitless—into whose hands do they fall?
Take care, Mr. Ren, holding the fishing pole!

[After speaking this verse, Hongzhi] then also raised a finger
and said, "Look!"

T. Cleary, *Book of Serenity*, p. 358.

41. "Seal" refers to the stamp of genuineness, also used for *mudrā*, a
meditative gesture or position. It is said that the ocean seal *samādhi*
is the consciousness from which Buddha spoke the Flower Ornament Sutra. A Huayen commentary says: "The 'ocean seal' is the
fundamental awareness of true thusness. When delusion ends, the
mind is clear and myriad forms simultaneously appear. It is like the
ocean. Due to wind there arise waves; if the wind stops the ocean is
calm and all images can reflect in it." Dōgen's essay "The Ocean
Seal Samādhi" begins, "In being Buddhas and Zen adepts, it is necessary to be the ocean seal *samādhi*" (T. Cleary, *Shōbōgenzō*, pp. 76,
78).

42. Zen Master Xuansha Shibei (835–908; "Dark Sand Complete
Teacher," in Japanese Gensha Shibi) said, "The entire universe is
one bright pearl." See Norman Waddell and Masao Abe, trans.,
"Dōgen's Ikka Myōju: One Bright Pearl," *Eastern Buddhist* 6, no. 2
(1971).

43. "This rustic [or humble] monk" refers to Hongzhi himself.

44. "Loom of energetic opportunity" is the translation for the character
ji (see note 39 above). The meaning "loom" is implied in this case by
its pairing with the character for "shuttle." This image indicates that
clear awareness cannot thoroughly penetrate until totalistic nona-
lienated vision has arisen or been enacted.

45. In Buddhism, "leaks" or "outflows" refer to attachment to sense objects and therefore to passions, as well as to the leakage of *samādhi*
energy.

46. A *nāga* is an ocean spirit or dragon, sometimes the guardian of Buddhist teachings not yet understandable in the human realm. *Nāga* meditation is meditation or *samādhi* in all times amid all activity.

47. Dongshan sometimes suggested that his disciples emulate the bird's trackless path through the sky, on which "one does not encounter a single person." He contrasted this to the original face, which he said was "not to follow the bird's path." The bird's path is an image for the monk's full functioning, leaving no traces, an image that goes back to Buddhist sutras, for example the Dhammapada and Prajñāpārāmitā. See Powell, *Record of Tung-shan*, pp. 55, 85.

48. This is a reference to Dongshan's "Song of the Jewel Mirror Samādhi": "Turning away and touching are both wrong, for it is like a mass of fire" (T. Cleary, *Timeless Spring*, p. 39).

49. Nirvana, the traditional Buddhist goal, is a state free of birth and death and conditioned consciousness. Here Hongzhi identifies nirvana with samsara, the conditioned realm of the creation of beings.

50. Case 67 of the *Book of Serenity*, "The Flower Ornament Sutra's Wisdom," quotes Shākyamuni Buddha's statement at his moment of enlightenment: "I now see all sentient beings everywhere fully possess the wisdom and virtues of the enlightened ones, but because of false conceptions and attachments they do not realize it" (T. Cleary, *Book of Serenity*, p. 281). See the section in the Introduction entitled "The Empty Field of Buddha Nature."

51. "Earth's dust" refers to worldly sense desires.

52. "Inside the gate" is a phrase for the teaching of a particular school; here Hongzhi refers to emerging from training to function freely. See also the poem "The Body Emerging from within the Gate" in the Religious Verses, below.

53. A quotation from Laozi's *Dao De Qing*, Book 41: "The great square has no corners. The greatest vessel takes the longest to finish. Great music has the faintest notes. The Great Form is without shape."

54. Bodhidharma (5th–6th century), the founder of Zen in China, told four of his disciples they had attained his skin, flesh, bones, and marrow, respectively. Since his successor, the Second Ancestor Dazu

Mirror," in Japanese Tokusan Senkan) is an Ancestor of the Yunmen and Fayan schools of Zen. Here "not a single dharma" means there is no teaching to give to anyone.

Religious Verses

1. This title could also be translated as "Admonitions for Zazen" or "The Point of Zazen." *Zazen* means seated meditation.
2. This verse recalls Dongshan's line from the "Song of the Jewel Mirror Samādhi": "When the wooden man begins to sing the stone woman gets up to dance," although the scene described here obviously precedes the wooden man's singing. See T. Cleary, *Timeless Spring*, p. 41. The River of Stars is the Milky Way.
3. See note 47 to the Practice Instructions.
4. The "four guests and hosts" is a teaching formulation by the great Linji Yixuan (d. 867), founder of the Rinzai school. See Chang, *Original Teachings of Ch'an Buddhism*, pp. 95−97.
5. The "truth body," or *dharmakāya*, is the absolute, empty, cosmic body of buddha.
6. The "response body," or transformation body or *nirmānakāya*, is the historical body of buddha incarnated in human form to respond to beings with awakened compassion.
7. Maitreya, predicted to be the next incarnate buddha, is said to be now residing in the heavens of the desire realm, waiting for the opportunity to appear and save all beings.
8. This famous expression by Linji denotes the totally accomplished adept. Hongzhi tells the story in the *Book of Serenity*: "Linji said to the assembly, 'There is a true man with no rank always going out and in through the portals of your face. Beginners who have not witnessed it, look! Look!' Then a monk came forward and said, 'What is the true man of no rank?' Linji got down from the seat, grabbed and held him: the monk hesitated. Linji pushed him away and said, 'The true man of no rank—what a piece of dry crap he is!'" (T. Cleary, *Book of Serenity*, case 38, p. 167).

9. "Memorial" means literally pagoda or stupa, a memorial structure housing the relics of a buddha or saint. Jianzhi Sengcan (d. 606), a leper, was still a layperson when he received the transmission from the Second Ancestor.

10. A quote from the popular long poem "On Faith in Mind," attributed to the Third Ancestor. See, for example, the translation in D. T. Suzuki, *Manual of Zen Buddhism* (New York: Grove Press, 1960), pp. 76–82.

11. Cave (*dong*) and cloud (*yun*) may well refer to the Sōtō founder, Dongshan Liangjie (807–869), and his successor, Yunju Daoying (d. 902), or perhaps Dongshan's teacher Yunyan Tansheng (781–841). See Introduction, "The Sōtō Context." Read thus, the last lines of this verse can be, "The stone ox roars! Dongshan and Yunju [or Yunyan] arose from this clarity."

12. Dayi Daoxin (580–651) was the first Zen ancestor to establish his own self-sufficient community. Huangmei is the place-name of the Fifth Ancestor, Daman (see following poem). This poem and the next refer to a story in the Sōtō tradition concerning the Fourth and Fifth Ancestors that is related by Dōgen in his "Shōbōgenzō Buddha Nature" essay (see the translation by Norman Waddell and Masao Abe in the *Eastern Buddhist* 8, no. 2 [1975]: 107–108). The story tells that the Fourth Ancestor, Dayi, encountered Daman in his previous life when he was called Zaisong Daozhe, "Planting Pines Wayfarer." Dayi said, "I would like to transmit the Dharma to you, but you are too old. If you get reborn into this world again, I will be waiting for you." Zaisong agreed. After he died and was reborn (as the person who would become the Fifth Ancestor), he encountered Dayi when he was seven years old and Dayi recognized him.

13. The Fifth Ancestor, Daman Hongren (602–675), established a large, thriving community. "Buddha nature is planted in different human births" is a continuing reference to the story related in the preceding note. At the time of the Fourth Ancestor Dayi's meeting with the seven-year-old Daman, an extraordinary dialogue ensued. Dayi asked him, "What is your name?" The boy replied, "There is a

name, but it is not an ordinary name." The Ancestor asked, "What name is it?" The boy said, "It is buddha nature." The Ancestor claimed, "You have no buddha nature." The unusual lad responded, "You say no [buddha nature] because buddha nature is emptiness." For Dōgen's equally extraordinary and enlightening commentary on this dialogue, see his "Buddha Nature" in ibid., pp. 108–112.

14. "The robe transmitted to the southern mountain range" is a reference to Daman's transmission to the southerner Dajian Huineng who became the Sixth Ancestor but had to flee to the south after receiving Daman's bequeathal. See notes 57–59 to the Practice Instructions. The western mountains, the direction of sunset, is a traditional Chinese image for death; "I can come again" thus refers to death and rebirth.

15. Touzi Yiqing (1032–1083) reestablished the Sōtō teaching after it had almost died out (see Appendix B, the Sōtō Lineage, note 2); he revived study of the five ranks in conjunction with the Flower Ornament Sutra. Relics of buddhas and saints kept in stupas usually consist of the remains of bones after the body's cremation, which are said to have a crystalline quality.

16. Furong Daokai (1043–1118) was Touzi's immediate successor and the teacher of Hongzhi's teacher Danxia Zichun. He revitalized and established enduring standards for the Sōtō monastic community. "Drumming and singing" is an image for the harmonious interaction of teacher and student.

17. In East Asia there is said to be a rabbit in the moon, as Westerners see a man in the moon.

18. The jade loom, which could also be translated as "jade machine" or "jade works," is an important image for Hongzhi for complete integration or simultaneous realization of both absolute and relative. In case 49 of the *Book of Serenity*, concerning Yunyan's statement to Dongshan, "Just this is it," Hongzhi's verse comment includes: "The jewel mirror, clear and bright, shows absolute and relative: the jade machine revolves—see them both show up at once." Wansong adds, "Although the mirror is clean, it has a back and a front; only the

jade works spinning it weaves them together, both light, both dark, with the technique of simultaneous realization" (from T. Cleary, *Book of Serenity*, p. 208).

19. "Upright" and "inclined" are synonyms for absolute and relative, or universal and particular. See the discussion of the five ranks in the Introduction, "The Sōtō Context."

20. *Sunyata*, Sanskrit for "emptiness," is the fundamental Buddhist teaching of the lack of inherent existence of all entities. It has also been translated as "relativity," as all entities are in reality interdependent and totally interconnected. *Mudrā* is Sanskrit for symbolic physical gestures or postures, often used in ritual enactments, which represent and actualize aspects of the teaching. *Mudrā* has been translated as "seal" in the sense of a confirmation or certification of a teaching. The zazen posture as a whole might be seen as a *mudrā*, and is so described with the ocean seal *samādhi*.

21. Reference here is to a story from the Warring States Period of China (480–221 B.C.E.). Mr. Ho presented a large rock containing jade to a ruler, who failed to recognize its value and ordered Ho's foot cut off. The rock was offered to a second ruler, who repeated the mistake, costing Ho his other foot. Finally a third ruler accepted the offering, appreciating its great value. See Burton Watson, trans., *Han Fei Tzu: Basic Writings* (New York: Columbia University Press, 1969), p. 80. Later this king arranged to trade the large jewel to a neighboring ruler for fifteen cities. The wise Minister Xiangru transported the rock for him. After handing over the jewel, Xiangru discerned that the rival king did not intend to honor his promise by giving the cities in exchange. Xiangru retrieved the large jewel by trickery: he pointed and said he would show the king a flaw in the rock; when the king handed the jewel back to Xiangru he safely fled back to his own land with the treasure.

22. Vimalakirti was an enlightened layman of Shākyamuni Buddha's time, much esteemed in Zen, who surpassed all the disciples and bodhisattvas in understanding. The climax of the sutra named after him is Vimalakirti's "thunderous" silence in response to the ques-

tion of how to enter nonduality, which follows numerous explanatory discourses on the subject by the assembled bodhisattvas. See Robert A. F. Thurman, trans., *The Holy Teachings of Vimalakīrti: A Mahāyāna Scripture* (University Park: Pennsylvania State University Press, 1976), pp. 73–77.

SELECTED
BIBLIOGRAPHY

Works in Chinese

Hongzhi Chan Shi Guang Lu [Extensive Record of Chan Master Hong-zhi]. In *Taishō Shinshū Daizōkyō*, no. 2001, vol. 48, pp. 73–78, 98–100. Tokyo: Taisho Issaikyō Kankōkai, 1924–1933.

Lao-Tzu: "My Words Are Very Easy to Understand." Lectures on the "Tao Teh Ching" by Man-jan Cheng. Original Chinese with translation by Tam C. Gibbs. Richmond, Calif.: North Atlantic Books, 1981.

Wu Deng Hui Yuan [Five Lamps Merged in the Source]. Edited by Dach-uan Puji, 13th century. Taipei: Guang Wen Bookstore, 1971.

Xu Chuan Deng Lu [Later Record of the Transmission of the Lamp]. Compiled by Yuan Chi, 14th century. In *Taishō Shinshū Daizōkyō*, no. 2077, vol. 51, p. 579. Tokyo: Taishō Issaikyō Kankōkai, 1924–1933.

Works in English

Abe, Masao. "Dōgen on Buddha Nature." *Eastern Buddhist* 4, no. 1 (1971).

Aitken, Robert, trans. *The Gateless Barrier: The Wu-men Kuan (Mumon-kan)*. San Francisco: North Point Press, 1990.

Badiner, Allan Hunt, ed. *Dharma Gaia: A Harvest of Essays on Buddhism and Ecology*. Berkeley: Parallax Press, 1990.

Bielefeldt, Carl. *Dōgen's Manuals of Zen Meditation*. Berkeley and Los Angeles: University of California Press, 1988.

Chang Chung-Yuan, trans. *Original Teachings of Ch'an Buddhism: Selected from "Transmission from the Lamp."* New York: Vintage Books, 1971.

Chang, Garma C. C. *The Practice of Zen*. New York: Perennial Library, 1959.

Cleary, J. C., trans. *Swampland Flowers: The Letters and Lectures of Zen Master Ta Hui*. New York: Grove Press, 1977.

————, trans. and ed. *Zen Dawn: Early Zen Texts from Tun Huang*. Boston: Shambhala, 1986.

Cleary, Thomas, trans. *The Book of Serenity*. Hudson, N.Y.: Lindisfarne Press, 1990.

————, trans. *The Buddhist "I Ching," by Chih-hsu Ou-i*. Boston: Shambhala, 1987.

————. *Entry into the Inconceivable: An Introduction to Hua Yen Buddhism*. Honolulu: University of Hawaii Press, 1983.

————, trans. *Entry into the Realm of Reality, the Guide: A Commentary on the "Gandhavyuha" by Li Tongxuan*. Boston: Shambhala, 1989.

————, trans. *The Flower Ornament Scripture: A Translation of the Avatamsaka Sutra*. 3 vols. Boston: Shambhala, 1983–1986.

————, trans. and ed. *The Inner Teachings of Taoism*. Boston: Shambhala, 1986.

————, trans. *Record of Things Heard: The "Shōbōgenzō Zuimonki," Talks of Zen Master Dōgen as Recorded by Zen Master Ejō*. Boulder, Colo.: Prajñā Press, 1980.

————, trans. *"Shōbōgenzō": Zen Essays by Dōgen*. Honolulu: University of Hawaii Press, 1986.

————, trans. *The Taoist I Ching*. Boston: Shambhala, 1986.

————, ed. and trans. *Timeless Spring: A Sōtō Zen Anthology*. Tokyo: Weatherhill, 1980.

————, trans. *Transmission of Light: Zen in the Art of Enlightenment by Zen Master Keizan*. San Francisco: North Point Press, 1990.

————, trans. *Zen Essence: The Science of Freedom*. Boston: Shambhala, 1989.

————, trans. *Zen Lessons: the Art of Leadership*. Boston: Shambhala, 1989.

Cleary, Thomas, and J. C. Cleary, trans. *The Blue Cliff Record*. 3 vols. Boulder, Colo.: Shambhala, 1977.

Cook, Francis. *How to Raise an Ox: Zen Practice as Taught in Zen Master Dōgen's "Shōbōgenzō."* Los Angeles: Center Publications, 1978.

Gimello, Robert M., and Peter N. Gregory, eds. *Studies in Ch'an and Hua Yen*. Honolulu: Kuroda Institute, University of Hawaii Press, 1983.

Heine, Steven. "Dōgen Casts Off 'What': An Analysis of Shinjin Datsuraku." *Journal of the International Association of Buddhist Studies* (Bloomington, Ind.) 9, no. 1. (1986).

Katagiri, Dainin. *Returning to Silence: Zen Practice in Daily Life*. Boston: Shambhala, 1988.

Kim, Hee Jin. *Dōgen Kigen: Mystical Realist*. Tucson: University of Arizona Press, 1975.

————, trans. *Flowers of Emptiness: Selections from Dōgen's "Shōbōgenzō."* Lewiston, N.Y.: Edwin Mellen Press, 1985.

Kodera, Takashi James. *Dōgen's Formative Years in China: An Historical Study and Annotated Translation of the "Hōkyō-ki."* Boulder, Colo.: Prajñā Press, 1980.

————. "Ta Hui Tsung-Kao (1089–1163) and His 'Introspecting the Kung-An Ch'an (Koan Zen).'" *Ohio Journal of Religious Studies* (Cleveland) 6, no. 1 (1978).

LaFleur, William R., ed. *Dōgen Studies*. Honolulu: Kuroda Institute, University of Hawaii Press, 1985.

Matsunaga, Daigan, and Alicia Matsunaga. *Foundation of Japanese Buddhism*. 2 vols. Los Angeles: Buddhist Books International, 1976.

Miura, Isshū, and Ruth Fuller Sasaki. *Zen Dust: The History of the Koan and Koan Study in Rinzai (Lin-chi) Zen.* New York: Harcourt, Brace & World, 1966. (Later republished, although without the voluminously comprehensive and invaluable footnotes, as *The Zen Koan: Its History and Use in Rinzai Zen.*)

Okumura, Shohaku, trans. and ed. *Dōgen Zen.* Kyoto: Kyoto Sōtō Zen Center, 1988.

————. *Shikantaza: An Introduction to Zazen.* Kyoto: Kyoto Sōtō Zen Center, 1985.

————, trans. *"Shōbōgenzō Zuimonki": Sayings of Eihei Dōgen Zenji, Recorded by Koun Ejō.* Kyoto: Kyoto Sōtō Zen Center, 1987.

Powell, William F., trans. *The Record of Tung-shan.* Honolulu: Kuroda Institute, University of Hawaii Press, 1986.

Price, A. F., and Mou-Lam Wong, trans. *The Diamond Sutra and the Sutra of Hui Neng.* Berkeley: Shambhala, 1969.

Seed, John, Joanna Macy, Pat Fleming, and Arne Naess. *Thinking Like a Mountain: Towards a Council of All Beings.* Philadelphia: New Society Publishers, 1988.

Sheng-Yen, Master. *Getting the Buddha Mind: On the Practice of Ch'an Retreat.* Elmhurst, N.Y.: Dharma Drum Publications, 1982.

————, trans. and ed. *The Poetry of Enlightenment: Poems by Ancient Ch'an Masters.* Elmhurst, N.Y.: Dharma Drum Publications, 1987.

Stevenson, Dan. "Silent Illumination Ch'an." *Ch'an Magazine* (Elmhurst, N.Y.) 2, no. 5 (1981).

Suzuki, Shunryu. *Zen Mind, Beginner's Mind.* New York: Weatherhill, 1970.

Tanahashi, Kazuaki, ed. *Moon in a Dewdrop: Writings of Zen Master Dōgen.* San Francisco: North Point Press, 1985.

Thurman, Robert A. F., trans. *The Holy Teachings of Vimalakīrti: A Mahāyāna Scripture.* University Park: Pennsylvania State University Press, 1976.

Verdu, Alfonso. *Dialectical Aspects in Buddhist Thought: Studies in Sino-Japanese Mahāyāna Idealism.* Lawrence: University of Kansas, Center for East Asian Studies, 1974.

Waddell, Norman, and Masao Abe, trans. "Dōgen's Fukanzazengi and Shōbōgenzō Zazengi." *Eastern Buddhist* 6, no. 2 (1973).

———, trans. "The King of Samādhis Samādhi: Dōgen's Shōbōgenzō Sammai Ō Zammai." *Eastern Buddhist* 7, no. 1 (1974).

———, trans. "Shōbōgenzō Buddha Nature." *Eastern Buddhist* 8, no. 2 (1975); 9, no. 1 (1976); 9, no. 2 (1976).

Wu, John C. H. *The Golden Age of Zen*. Taipei: United Publishing Center, 1975.

Wu, Yi. *The Book of Lao Tzu*. San Francisco: Great Learning Publishing Company, 1989.

———. *Chinese Philosophical Terms*. Lanham, Md.: University Press of America, 1986.

———. *The Mind of Chinese Ch'an (Zen): The Ch'an School Masters and Their Kung-ans*. San Francisco: Great Learning Publishing Company, 1989.

Yamada, Koun, trans. *Gateless Gate*. Los Angeles: Center Publications, 1979.

Yampolsky, Philip B., ed. and trans. *The Platform Sutra of the Sixth Patriarch*. New York: Columbia University Press, 1967.

Yukoi, Yūhō, trans. *The Shōbōgenzō*. Tokyo: Sankibō Buddhist Bookstore, 1986.

———, with Daizen Victoria. *Zen Master Dōgen: An Introduction with Selected Writings*. Tokyo: Weatherhill, 1976.

Casey

June - Aug
10 weeks

Job   15-20 hr ~~pw work~~

5 weeks May 16 -
         June 24

14
14   6 wchs June 25 -
9   Aug 7

37   4 weeks Aug 8 -
                   Aug 30
   15

  (52)   5 miles base
    0
                        10 mile long

I don't give myself, open to work
doesn't allow me to grow

① Shoes

┌──────────────┐
│ tempo   │ 2 weeks   30 ish
│ long run   │ 3-4 weeks 40 ish
│ training runs│ 4-5 week   50 ish
└──────────────┘
                  4 weeks   58 ish
|

THE TRANSLATORS

TAIGEN DANIEL LEIGHTON has been engaged in formal Sōtō Zen practice since 1975 with both Japanese and American teachers. He is an ordained priest in the lineage of Shunryu Suzuki Roshi, and was head monk at Tassajara Zen Mountain Center. Leighton has a B.A. from Columbia College, New York, and received an M.A. in Buddhist Studies from the California Institute of Integral Studies in San Francisco.

He was a co-translator of *Moon in a Dewdrop: Writings of Zen Master Dōgen* with Kazuaki Tanahashi, with whom he also collaborated on published translations of poems by the Japanese monk Ryōkan and the early Chinese master Shitou. Leighton is also an award-winning documentary film and tape editor. He currently resides in Kyoto, Japan.

YI WU, a scholar of Chinese culture, religion, and philosophy, received a Ph.D. from the University of Chinese Culture in Taipei, where he was chairman of the Department of Philosophy. He is currently Professor of Chinese Language in the Philosophy and Religion Department of the California Institute of Integral Studies in San Francisco.

Yi Wu has published fourteen books in Chinese, and designed a radio series in Taiwan about Chinese philosophy. In English, he has published *Chinese Philosophical Terms*, *The Book of Lao Tzu*, and *The Mind of Chinese Ch'an (Zen)*.

may 22   Kare Ku

quib

stuff
finals

June 14   ESG or
           Swamp Rub

↑
I'll be gone

Fri-Sun
finals

mom's b'day

carl   Junior

team meets

W   bucket
     pants

trac
picnic

R   paper
     portfolio   Fri   BAT/SUN
                        another day
philo   /evaluate   labs   brunch
lottery prom   due

North
Durham
Carnegie

Design by David Bullen
Typeset in Mergenthaler Fournier
by Wilsted & Taylor
Printed by Maple-Vail
on acid-free paper

experience leads baseball cards
to enlighten organize stuff

Happy = Buddhism ?

why is it sitting   wise girl
no one   with strong opinions
knows   perspective backed by experience
No meaning of life   despite disagreeing
no right way   no fight back
to   losing the argument
evaluate   losing my self
                         she pushes me down
No proof   walking away
                                  hers
                         she came in   I try to
I thought it   my heart fluttered about start-
was working   needing companionship   over
                         needing love
                         not necessarily her
                         but what she gives

hide in ministry

or is it me